BAREFOOT + DOCTOR'S
HANDBOOK
FOR HEROES

BAREFOOT ✛ DOCTOR'S
HANDBOOK
FOR HEROES

PIATKUS

Edited and inspired by Jamie Catto

© 1999 Barefoot Doctor, Stephen Russell

First published in 1999 by
Judy Piatkus (Publishers) Ltd
5 Windmill Street, London W1P 1HF

A catalogue record for this book is available from the British Library

ISBN 0–7499–1981–7

Edited by Kirsty Fowkes
Designed by the Senate
Illustrations by Roger O'Reilly/Folio

Typeset by Action Publishing Technology Ltd, Gloucester

Printed and bound in Great Britain

Dedication

To Russell-The-Spiritual-Firefighter (Russell Ward) and everyone with the imagination, wit and sheer audacity to walk their own path: the new heroes of the twenty-first century.

Impressive quotation

'... who might dare to afford the whole range and wealth of being natural, being strong enough for such freedom; the man of tolerance, not from weakness but from strength, because he knows how to use to his advantage even that from which the average nature would perish; the man for whom there is no longer anything that is forbidden – unless it be *weakness*, whether it be called vice or virtue.'

Friedrich Nietzsche

List of Contents

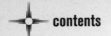

contents

⟡ contents

✦ contents

Longest sentence in the book (probably the world)

Handbook For Heroes, a spiritual guide to fame and fortune, is for everyone no matter their age, gender, creative persuasion, religious/spiritual belief system, sexual orientation, race, culture, wealth levels, social standing, celebrity status, profession, job; whether employed, self-em-ployed/freelance, employer of others, tycoon, aristocrat, fallen aristocrat, jumped-up working boy/girl, no matter their musical taste or dress-sense, who wishes to maximise their personal hero-potential and in so doing attain the (dubious) pleasures of fame and fortune by perceptually reframing their experience of everyday working reality in a spiritual/magical context according to the time-honoured precepts of an ancient (Chinese) Taoist concept known as mastering the Five Excellences, and is presented in such a way as to facilitate your opening the book at any page at random for on-the-spot oracular advice/guidance appertaining to where you are at that very moment in time and space, but which can also be read sequentially in traditional book-reading style, one page at a time if the desire takes you, to follow the thought track of the enigmatic author, himself a contemporary hero of modern Taoist folklore, currently possessed of just enough units of fame and fortune to dare think he knows what he's talking about, or at least make a good scam of it, who is well enough versed in the Taoist arts with twenty years' professional experience as a healer, teacher and communicator, whose media mission is to demystify and make ancient, arcane knowledge/secrets available on a mass scale for maximum consumer utilisation, in order to promote greater general relaxation levels for everyone on the planet at this time and for the benefit of (hopefully) future generations, and who has a schoolboy-like propensity for playing with sentence structure and length for your amusement and his own, but who remains throughout, your cheeky/chi (ki), liberty-taking but genuinely good-natured Barefoot Doctor.

Straight
In

DISCLAIMER AND POLITE WARNING

This Handbook is a complete con and the author an out-and-out con man.

Reading this material will *not* bring you fame and fortune.

It *may* do that for me.

Fortunately what I have to write about fits into the category of useful information. Information which if taken and used will *cert*ainly give you that extra portion of 'magic' you may need to actualise your daydreams. Simply reading it won't do that.

That's partly why I say the book's a con.

But it's also because I wish to introduce you immediately to the idea that all human interaction is one big con, as in confidence-game. You can achieve everything you want providing you have the correct tools (skills) and *con*–fidence (literally keeping the faith with yourself), i.e. *if you believe you can, you can.*

If I'm confident enough to write the book confidently, which in turn inspires the publishers with enough confidence to invest in it and market it confidently, the PR people enough to plug it, and the booksellers enough to display it, then there's a good chance that you'll have the confidence to invest your money, time, mental energy and shelf space in it, too.

Here I sit, poised on the edge of freefall waffle and, lest I take that pointless tumble, let me put it simply:

Everyone wants to be famous. At least once. And why not? It's fun. Anyone who's famous'll tell you that.

Everyone wants a fortune. It's the currency of the game we play here.

Everyone wants to be a hero (or anti-hero) and has a potential hero within.

Everyone likes to think of themselves as being a bit spiritual these days, especially when in pursuit of fame and fortune.

So, good title. Mountains of information carried in ten words and a bit of graphic design. And if you add to that the author's name: enigmatic,

mysterious, vaguely ethnic, trippy, hippy, healery, the a.k.a of th
hardest-working man in chi-business, a man with a bit of a reputation a
a cosmic lad about town, occasional womaniser and spiritual bad-bo
guru with a risqué sense of humour and a thorough self-knowing of h
onions – you're looking at a product. A product which I guarantee wi
bring you fame and fortune (to some degree), if you use the informatio
and don't just read it. Anyone can be famous. Anyone can be wealth
You don't need special genes. You simply need to tap into your ow
innate hero-nature.

That's the purpose of this Handbook, to show you how to do it. Liste
– but decide for yourself.

So that's the score: the book's a con, I'm a con man, but a positive cc
man with something of substance to impart, with a cheeky penchant f
leading you a little bit hither and thither, a liberty I know, but that's th
nature of this fame and fortune business for us heroes. It'll lead you
right merry dance if you don't stay centred. That (centring) and mar
other fine tricks only fit for heroes on the quest for f'n'f will be reveale
as the material opens up.

*Please be aware that neither I, the publishers, nor indeed any party involved
the chain of events culminating in the possession on your part of the enclos
material, can or will be held responsible for any damage to your person, phys
cal, psychic, spiritual, emotional, financial or otherwise, arising fro
experiments you may conduct based on the said enclosed material.*

Furthermore, I feel honour-bound to add that like *Handbook For The Urb*
Warrior, *Handbook For Heroes* is a disguised propaganda-vehicle throug
which the author again propounds the tenets of Wayward Taoism, th
main dictum of which is, *'Do whatever you like (providing no harm to anoth*
is intended) and not only get away with it, but be loved for it even more!', th
propagation of which he believes will help people, and which he inten
to further because he's not the messiah (he's a very naughty boy) [s
Wayward Taoism p.21].

So, that's me. I'm clean. (America's covered.) You're probably already little confused. But what the hell. Read on ...

ou must be mad

know I am.) Isn't it enough that you've managed to make it here today? n't it ample sustenance for your soul simply to know you've survived he (approx.) twelve point three thousand dangers that have threatened our well-being each and every day since you were born?

(Did you know?) you're on a ball of gas-filled rock hurtling through he void at *nineteen miles a second* to goodness-knows-where, your very xistence at the whim of comets, viruses, ecological meltdown, socio- olitical breakdown, warmongers, rapists and gangstas, not to mention lobal economic collapse and yet you were calm and collected enough to op whatever else you were doing just now and grace these humble ages with your precious attention. And why?

Because you must be stark raving mad.

You could be getting on with your life quietly now, keeping your head own, not making waves, having an easy time of it. But not you.

You wanted fame. You wanted fortune. An ordinary humdrum life asn't good enough for you. Not simply satisfied to have survived so far, gainst all the odds, you're crazy enough to push the envelope that little t further and risk your life for this, the quest of f'n'f.

What do you think you are? A bloody hero?

Answer: *yes*.

u're a bloody hero and I'm Barefoot Doctor

bviously, I'm a bloody hero too (I use this adjective partly to indulge in e vernacular, partly in irony, and partly literally, as in sanguine or filled ith blood/vim and vigour). If you've read *Handbook For The Urban arrior*, you'll have noticed me impartially described on the sleeve as 'a ntemporary hero of Taoist folklore'. It's a fact. (It's in print.) Barefoot octor is a hero.

If you haven't read *Handbook For The Urban Warrior* yet, I strongly rec- mmend you consider it. Not just because I'm a cross-marketing and omotion fiend, not just for the dollar I'll earn, but because I (along with a rapidly, exponentially expanding circle of other nutters) think it's damn fine read. As well as being a 'complete' spiritual survival guide an a good laugh, *Handbook For The Urban Warrior* also provides the basi upon which *Handbook For Heroes* stakes its own claim to fame and fortune In other words, reading the first Handbook will greatly enhance you understanding, enjoyment and appreciation of this one.

The glitzy, shimmering rewards of fame and fortune recently acquire by my heroic self as a result of twenty-one-and-a-half-years' consister questing on the path, suddenly breaking through critical mass levels short while before publication of the first Handbook [see *Persistence of th hero* p.33], have given me a new and decidedly stronger perspective fro which to present you these old Taoist secrets for acquiring fame an fortune in a new Taoist way.

By trade, as well as being a compulsive writer/communicator, I'm als a compulsive healer, spiritual teacher, martial arts instructor, musicia general miscreant and media tart. I feel no need to pound out further cre dentials on my keys. Let it suffice to say that I've been working in th field (of living theatre) consistently for over twenty-three years and cor sider myself competent at what I do. Them's my credentials. This is m written voice, and I'm happy and privileged to be talking to you with i

My intention is to convey important information with optimum cor sumer utilisation factor, and have a damn good laugh doing it. Hope yo on the receiving end have one too and pick up some top tips in th process.

Well, I think I've indulged quite enough in this sentimental preambl so without further ado let us hasten towards the main body of inform tion herein on offer.

Isn't spiritual fame and fortune a paradox?

Depends on your concept of spirituality.

If your path is one of renunciation and austerity, then you real shouldn't be looking at this book anyway. Put it down straight away, le you be quickly corrupted. If, however, your spiritual path tips more the liberal side of things, like mine (Path of the Wayward Taoist), the you're set to have a (spiritual) ball with this information. (Please note th

aoist spiritual methods are universal and do not conflict with, and
ndeed may be used alongside, those of any other spiritual path.)

Spirit is ubiquitous and universal. It's everywhere, all at once,
hroughout time, space and matter for ever and ever. Nothing could exist
vithout it. That's just how it is for me and I'm not interested in justifying
t. Every illusion thrown out by the magic lantern – that is, everything we
ee including you and me – has the basis for its existence in spirit. Even,
nd sometimes especially, the grand illusion of fame and fortune.

So, if f'n'f is where your fascination takes you, go there with awareness
nd that's where you'll receive the lessons you need to grow. These
essons will probably occur with similar frequency, intensity and general
ontent as if you were a renunciate (monk or nun). The only difference
vill be the local scenery. The path of fame and fortune will obviously be
nore colourful and probably a lot more fun, but will be just as painful,
naybe more so [see *The hero's pain* p.36].

Once you've started on the spiritual path you can't get off. It makes no
difference how you dress up the scenery or with whom you choose to
njoy it. The lessons your guiding spirit wishes to set up for you along the
vay will be the lessons you get. Whether they come through the abbot in
mountain monastery or the critic in the morning papers, your lessons
vill be the same in essence. And when I say lessons, I mean signposts to
uide you home. And when I say home, I don't mean your hyse in
slington or your loft in Soho, I mean, and you may have to use your
magination for this, that state of undifferentiated oneness and every-
hing-about-you-joined-upness akin to which you probably felt in the
vomb, and which you are now seeking to regenerate and perpetuate in
he quest for f'n'f.

Because when you taste the fame, when you find yourself standing at
hat tastefully lit Beverly Hills poolside party talking to this or that film-
tar friend of yours, and you can discipline yourself to see through the
litz to the reality of the cohesive spirit behind the scenes, you are effec-
vely spiritualising the profane, which is the best you can hope for,
piritually speaking in this tawdry paradise we inhabit.

So, no paradox in the idea of fame and fortune being a spiritual busi-
ess. QED.

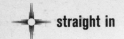

What are barefoot doctors?

Humble healers going literally barefoot, romantically padding about the countryside of China and South-East Asia since ancient times. Now mostly extinct. (The title has coincidentally also been adopted in post cultural-revolution China by unromantic conveyor-belt-style rural medics.)

Most of the more well-loved barefoot doctors of the past couple of centuries have been women, a fact that this Barefoot Doctor finds titillating if not gratifying, being possessed of a well-developed feminine side as he is, though being also a compulsive heterosexual, and feels privileged to be an honorary member of this particular society.

Barefoot doctors are able to fix people up in most cases, no matter the condition, using just the energy coming through their bare(foot) hands, that is, without tools. In more extreme cases they use acupuncture, massage, herbs, bone cracking, joint stretching as well as Taoist versions of modern psychotherapy and hypnotherapy, and quasi-shamanistic practices.

All these modalities and more are employed extensively by this Barefoot Doctor who treats an average of seventy people each week when not otherwise engaged in creative pursuits such as writing this Handbook or teaching classes in the ways of urban warriors and heroes and who, working habitually barefoot, inherited this cute moniker when a respected journalist he was treating looked at his naked feet, laughed and renamed him thus. (So it must be good.)

It's like calling yourself Cab Driver if you drive a cab, Actor if you work in a bar, or Psychic Taxidermist if you … well, you get my drift. As well as being catchy, it provides the author with a private identity, i.e. his own name and is a useful outlet for any underlying schizophrenic tendencies.

People generally call me the Doc. Feel free to think of me in that intimate light while reading this Handbook. After all I already take that liberty of intimacy with you.

What is a handbook?

A book which springs easily to hand, fits easily in your hand and falls open easily in your hands. The last of these can be effected in three ways:

You can follow the material in linear sequential style, as in page one followed by page two and so on.

You can select topics at will, assisted by the contents list at the front end and index at the rear end.

Or you can employ random selection method (RSM) which involves allowing the book to open up where it will. This can be augmented by a preliminary manual flick of the pages. RSM lends itself to effective oracular use, by simply holding a particular situation in your mind's eye, allowing the Handbook to fall open and whichever phrase or concept jumps into your field of vision first will usually hold the answer for you. Obviously this won't always work but what do you want for ten quid?

Whichever of these you choose, your reading experience can be greatly augmented by frequently provided cross-referencing as you go along.

Hero/ine

Someone brave who protects and preserves life of self and, more relevantly, of others, in the face of overwhelming odds.

In the face of spiralling global insanity, the hero through the power of meditation remains centred and calm and teaches others likewise [see *Meditation* p.126]. This is the protection or preservation of calm, i.e. sanity, the more of which exists, the more chance there'll be for (unmutated human) life to perpetuate itself.

In the face of physical danger from out-of-control humans, the hero, through the power of martial art, protects self and others often without a single fist flung or shot fired [see *The Five Excellences* p.121 and *Martial arts* p.138].

In the face of disease, the hero, through the power of healing [see *The Five Excellences* p.121 and *Healing* p.155], can prolong the lifespan and alleviate suffering of self and others.

In the face of cultural dullness and potential mediocrity, the hero, through the power of composition [see *The Five Excellences* p.121, *Compositional skills* p.170 and *Following your creative impulses* p.98] manifests great artistic works, to protect self and others from spiritual ennui, i.e. boredom.

In the face of blandness and stale amateurism, through the power of presentation [see *The Five Excellences* p.121 and *Presentation skills* p.180], the hero brings produce to market perfectly packaged and wrapped thus preserving for us the finesse and freshness of life mirrored in art.

In the context of fame and fortune, a hero is anyone courageous/outrageous enough to risk everything to make their lives sparkle both outside and in with colour and excitement, not just for themselves but for everyone in their world to enjoy and be edified by.

Alternatively, someone whose parents/family/teachers/peers have miraculously managed not to fuck up, possessed of rare and perfect inner and outer beauty and proportions, good muscle tone, clear skin, soothing/rousing/pleasing voice, cheerful and positive spirit, kindly and compassionate disposition, no discernible character or personality defects, integrity, dignity, valour, bravery, nobility, honesty and modesty, who's altogether so superhumanly magnificent that you can't even feel envy and for whom you can only feel deepest admiration and total respect.

The likelihood of that, however, is slim (no offence), but if, in fact, you currently find yourself thus and can verify same with three honest friends (you too-good-to-be-true bastard), you're obviously only reading this now for mild titillative purposes and should know better.

Spiritual

Chanting om to yourself (quietly) while standing in line at the cashpoint.

Talking softly to your favourite deity while having a manicure.

Praying hard to Shiva then detonating five nuclear bombs in succession, deep inside the Himalayas, triggering an earthquake five days later in Bolivia.

Praying hard to Allah then doing likewise triggering an earthquake two days later in Afghanistan.

Seeing through the surface of every phenomenon, including persons (including your own), animals, plantlife, minerals (including planets), suns and suchlike, and through every situation encountered to the underlying/overlying, surrounding and wholly connective etheric tissue of ubiquitous, all-seeing, all-hearing, all-tasting, all-smelling, all-touching spirit; on seeing through to this depth/height of reality, marvelling at the constant and continual generative power of your personal universe, and feeling so happy and bright that you choose to remember to remind yourself constantly of its ineffable presence, not for its sake (it doesn't give a damn) but for yours. And in so doing, you carry that awareness with love into everything you're doing, all the time, no matter what.

That's spiritual.

Guide

Someone who, not having a lover or any other reason to stay in bed, got up while you were still asleep and trekked up the early morning mountain to the peak, kindly painting red arrows on the rocks to point out the way for you when you're ready to smack the trail.

The way is not without its dangers and the red arrows do not constitute a safety net. Every trekker has to take responsibility for his/her own journey to the peak and is free to stop and turn back at any time.

There are many ways to walk up a mountain. This particular guide is of the Wayward Taoist School [see *Wayward Taoism* p.21], specifically following the method of mastering the Five Excellences [see *The Five Excellences* p.121].

Actually there is no mountain save in your imagination, so onward with the book, which gets more interesting the higher you go (towards the peak!).

Fame

The phenomenon of other people, many of whom you've never met, talking about you and your business as if it's their own, projecting fantasies on to you of a more or less wholesome/accurate nature and psychologically appropriating you or their idea of you as a fixture in their internal/imaginary map of the universe.

Paradoxically, however famous you become, you can never experience your own fame. You can never be there in person, unless heavily disguised or sequestered in a closet when they talk about you, without altering the chemistry and dynamics of the situation.

You can experience the effects of your fame, both positive and negative, turning heads in a restaurant, people presuming to invade your privacy as you walk out of a shop, but not the essence of your fame itself.

Fame arises either from birth (into a famous family), through marriage, by association, through excelling in your chosen field of endeavour, championing a worthy cause, packaging yourself, i.e. your gifts in an exceptionally successful and culturally relevant way, having a good PR person or any combination of the above.

There is useless or insubstantial fame, where you literally use the fame for nothing but being famous.

There is useful or substantial fame where you use your influence to promote a cause you deem worthy along with any associated products or merchandise arising thereof, the taking up of which is intended to generally alleviate suffering and ameliorate life on Earth for others.

Handbook For Heroes is concerned with the latter [see *Degrees of fame and fortune* p.73].

Fortune

That which you receive when you successfully package the essence of your particular gift into a product which the marketplace takes up eagerly and dispenses units thereof to sufficient numbers of people/punters spread over a large enough area for an adequate amount of time for you eventually to encounter a tax situation/problem and set about investigating offshore banking facilities.

This often arises when adequate levels of fame have been established to stimulate sufficient demand.

Fortune is an immensely spiritual phenomenon. Many fine goddesses have wandered the Elysian fields of various people's cosmologies throughout the ages, devoting themselves exclusively to the caretaking and dispensing of it to attest to this. Among these are Kuan Yin (China), Lakshmi (India), Fortuna (Italy), for example. Talking to them personally about your financial requirements can often yield instantaneous benefits [see *Fortuna, Lakshmi, Kuan Yin and you* p.84].

Fortune is the bounty of the heavenly realms made manifest for you on Earth. Along with fame, it is merely the froth on the champagne and must not be worshipped or adored as the spiritual substance of life itself.

Further warning concerning the illusory nature of fame and fortune

Neither fame nor fortune will touch the essence of who you are. Fame will colour your experience of the party by expanding the circle of interesting/dull people who wish to meet you and hang out with you. You won't find yourself standing like a lemon on your own for long, you won't care so much if you do, and you'll always have the dubious satisfaction of knowing that you're an object of interest. This is unlikely to produce more than froth on the champagne of your private/personal life, i.e. it's unlikely you'll make any deep, lasting friendships from it. But don't be closed to it, 'cause you never know.

Fortune, often resulting from a combination of fame, having a good product/package to sell, and marketing it effectively, though more tangible an illusion than fame, is nevertheless an illusion and like fame will not touch the essence of who you are. Fortune merely affects the levels of physical comfort you experience at home and when travelling. This includes the quality of the location of your home/s and/or hotel rooms/suites etc., your furnishings and furniture at home and while travelling, tools and equipment [see *The importance of having a good tool* p.194], clothing, seating arrangements on planes, boats, trains, and in cars, as well as the quality of the food you eat and often the views you enjoy, but will not touch your soul, except in as much as you spend time consciously revelling in the heavenly grace that comes with appreciation of your fortune. If you're feeling miserable, pleasant surroundings, when you get used to them, will only provide the backdrop to your misery and will not ease your internal suffering [see *Healing* p.155].

Fame and fortune are as much an illusion as ignomy and impoverishment, not that many people caught in the illusion of either extreme would agree. It all passes the instant you die. So if you're going to pick an illusion and you're partial to the odd splash of colour and warmth, you might derive greater pleasure from f'n'f than i'n'i. It's all a question of which game you want to play while you're hanging around preparing to die.

Fortune and fame are just a game and not salvation by another name.

Neither fame nor fortune will save you from your existential crisis. The

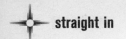 **straight in**

only thing that will ease your passage through that one is cultivating your spiritual connection to Creation [see *Meditation* p.126].

The manifestation of fame and fortune is just a game you play while you go about the business of mastering yourself in the pursuit of getting your message across. It's like doodling while talking on the phone. Other than ensuring optimum perception management (PR) and financial balance maintenance at all times, it's best not to pay f'n'f too much attention [see *Importance of PR (perception management)* p.200 and *Opening bank accounts as receptacles* p.208].

You're already famous with your mother, at least. All you have to do is expand on that

To your mum or whoever weened you off the teet and into the world, you're famous. You played an enormous part in reshaping and redefining her role in her own life story. I hope you fulfilled your role as weenee graciously enough to be a hero, as opposed to anti-hero in her eyes. If not and you find yourself stuck repeatedly acting out anti-heroic parts in the play [see *Living theatre* p.40], that's fine, too, as long as you can find a way to package and market it effectively.

As you've probably discovered for yourself, once you're famous with one person, you can rapidly expand your sphere of fame/infamy by joining up at your local kindergarten and so on through school, university, travelling, working at jobs, etc. until you arrive at the present degree of fame/infamy you currently enjoy/disenjoy. Right now, as we speak, others are probably talking about you (and me – you'd better stop phoning!). Perhaps it's just your friends and acquaintances indulging in gossip. Perhaps it's Fifi/Bert telling their friends what a great fuck you are.

Now, if you want to increase that effect in order to attract fortune in your direction, all you have to do is formulate a worthwhile message and dedicate your life to getting it across, initially among those with whom you're already famous/infamous who, if sufficiently inspired by it, will proceed unbidden, each in their own way, to talk about you to others outside the initial circle, who in turn may do likewise, thus spreading your fame in exponentially expanding circles to the extent you got your act right [see *Presentation skills* p.180].

The degree of fortune you require depends entirely on your imagination. There are no limits to what you can 'have'. You cannot own anything in reality, as everything you own stays behind when you die, so you can only caretake. But being part of the Tao [see *The Tao* p.21], you are entitled to sharing, i.e. enjoying everything that exists.

Because many others are playing the game too, however, there are long queues for most of the more popular rides, hence you will have to develop patience [see *Persistence of the hero* p.33] in the quest for fortune attainment.

Start with whatever degree of fortune you currently caretake. Even if you're all the way down near zero, you at least have this Handbook to caretake, and that's a good start. Most of us, however, are managing to manifest more props than this. Consider the amount of fortune you actually caretake right now, however low or high the degree, and say 'thank you'. To proceed from here, all you need is to expand on the degree of fortune you 'have'.

This will occur naturally of itself as you follow and practice absolutely everything in this Handbook. That's all you have to do!

the
meat 1
Heroes

THE TAO

Imagine every living creature, ectoplasmic and bioplasmic, every life form, every star, black hole and any other aggregate of matter, gases or energy, as well as every thought, word, action, feeling, event and interaction that has ever occurred, will ever occur and is occurring right now even as we speak, throughout time and space in every possible dimension for ever and ever, is an animated, integrated working part of one huge mother of a universal mind/consciousness that knows everything, sees everything, creates everything, sustains everything, destroys everything, rebuilds it again and doesn't give a fuck. That's not the Tao, the Tao is entirely ineffable, but it's a damn good pop at an explanation.

Taoism

A collection of psychophysical methods originated in ancient China for attaining and sustaining health and peace of mind by entering a perpetual state of meditative awareness. This hangs on a philosophy based on following the natural flow of events in your life according to the concept of yin and yang, the daily practice of which develops a superhuman brand of energy or 'chi'. Chi provides you with the power to heal yourself and others and is the quasi-alchemical agent which connects you to the invisible world of spirit in order that your wishes be made magically manifest.

Wayward Taoism

Doing whatever you can get away with.
Moving constantly wayward, as in risking all to follow the way or Tao of your personal adventure.

Barefoot Doctor's modern-day brand of Taoism which, though firmly adhering to the principles of traditional Taoism, holds no pre-set rules or traditions sacrosanct and draws its inspiration from the source of all being, the Tao, in exactly the same way as did the first Taoists, thus ensuring freshness and authenticity at all times.

Specifically here, it is concerned with providing you, the hero, with a context for integrating Chinese Taoist methods for health, wealth, longevity and peace with the bad habits you've picked up.

BACKDROP TO THE HERO'S ADVENTURE

You are witnessing the deconstruction of a paradigm (commonly held belief in the structure and nature of reality as we see it). The effects of this are the universally visible signs of apparent probable breakdown and transformation of most ecological, biological, geological, social, moral, political, geo-political, financial, economic, religious (other than funda-mentalist) and spiritual systems on Earth.

Emerging majestically, as yet invisible to the untrained eye, from within the debris of the old is a new paradigm, its roots buried in ground far more ancient than that of the present one, and its branches extending outwards into so far unknown realms to manifest as who knows what.

Whether we experience this unfoldment or revelation as humans or cockroaches is a matter of pure conjecture at this stage of the game.

Missiles may fly, the planetary axis tilt, plague and disease run rampant and mass psychosis take hold, but you, the hero, walk on undaunted, staring danger, death and dissolution in the face with a level gaze. You're so centred, calm and focused on your adventure, you actu-ally welcome a backdrop of potentially spiralling chaos because it adds poignancy to your personal story. If everything were peace and plenty and no dangers existed to threaten survival, heroes would become an obsolete irrelevance. As it is, your relevance has never been so strong nor your contribution so urgently necessary.

Addressing all boy-heroes and girl-heroes (heroines) alike

It almost goes without saying, except I have to, that the title, 'Hero', in this Handbook, is intended to apply equally to male and female heroes. Use of the more archaic title, 'heroine', has been mostly eschewed for the sake of economy but this in no way implies a propensity for members of either gender to be more heroic than the other. (That's me sorted with the sisters.)

Advantages of being a hero

You don't have to live a humdrum life out in the suburbs. (You can if you want to and be the hero waiting for the call, biding your time under the pretence of living a humdrum life out in the suburbs, but you don't have to, so why bother?)

You enjoy the hero's global view and freedom and recognise no boundary preventing you from actualising your master-scheme.

Your life is so exciting that you never even consider spending any of it watching TV or amusing yourself with mindless games.

Your personal power is so strong that you never need the approval of others to make your decisions [see *Making Decisions – pendulums, Tarot, I Ching* p.61] and are able to stand confidently alone without other people's expectations and madness crowding your thoughts [see *Meditation* p.126].

You get all the girls/boys (depending on gender and preference).

You never get stuck in a rut because you're always moving on in your adventure.

Your life makes a positive difference to the soup.

Disadvantages of being a hero

You can't live a 'normal', humdrum life out in the suburbs. (You can try and pretend you're the hero waiting for the call, but your global vision and need for freedom will drive you to distraction, not letting you rest until you start actualising your master-scheme.)

Your life is so exciting/busy, you don't even get time to sit down and watch TV or play mindless games on your computer.

Your personal power is so strong and your decision-making process which determines your path so well tuned that you become part of a rarefied species and have to cope with huge chunks of time spent alone [see *Loneliness of the hero* p.32].

You get all the girls/boys (driving you mad).

You may never get to put down roots because you're always moving on in your adventure.

Your life makes a positive difference to the soup but you may never get time to sit down and savour it properly and are subject to bouts

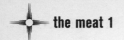

of angst when your hero's global vision indicates the possibility of the entire soup bowl being tipped up and thrown in the gutter.

Hero vs. anti-hero

One person's hero is another's anti-hero. You may be a hero in one social sector or stratum and a villain in another [see *You can please some of the people some of the time* p.103]. The matter is rarely settled even long after your death and the rationale for judging you one way or the other is based entirely on spurious, subjective criteria.

But you're a hero, so you don't give a damn [see *Being your own hero* p.35].

Motivations for being a hero

These possible motivations are mentioned merely as a trigger to evoke a response in you and provoke you to examine your own motivations and do not in any way comprise either a comprehensive list or an inadvertent insight into the author's own personal set of motivations.

You are impelled by an overwhelming/underlying altruistic, creation-adoring urge to alleviate suffering and enhance life however and wherever you encounter it.
You feel an uncontrollable urge to map out the way for others.
You watch hero movies and read hero stories and identify heavily with the archetypal hero figure.
You are fully aware that you are living tenuously on the surface of a planet which is rotating on its own axis at one thousand miles an hour while simultaneously travelling around the sun at sixty-six thousand miles an hour through what amounts to outer space on a journey of unknown destination, without knowing why, and that to respond in anything less than full heroic fashion would simply be bad cosmic manners.
You happen upon this Handbook by chance having hitherto had no interest in being a hero and decided through sheer boredom/ wanting something to read on the loo, to direct your energies towards mastering various life skills suggested in this Handbook,

which you hope will enable your output to reflect the awesome significance of your place in time and space rather than distract
meaninglessly from it.

You feel that anything less than a hero's path would be too limiting
a focus for your lifetime's endeavours.

You were always a natural hero amongst your peers from the time
you first mixed with others of your own age and know no other way
to be.

You got bored being a non-hero and, noticing the world might come
to an end any day now, you thought you'd try something new while
there was still time.

You find the mass hypnosis of televised, electronic culture too limiting and are impelled to do something different to push the
envelope.

Fictionalising your life

To be a hero you have to see your life as a fiction and yourself as a fic-
tional character. This is a spiritual/metaphysical operation involving
reframing your life as you have seen it up till now in the context of a
romantic, global adventure story.

This makes your moment-to-moment experience of life no less real. To
the contrary, it makes it more so. When you're stuck with the notion that
your life as you've seen it up until now is an indisputable fact, you're
automatically trapped in the world of distinctions and relativity caused
by limited perception.

Your perceptions are a product of taking the evidence of the world you
see around you and running it through the various filters you have
unconsciously constructed according to more or less faulty guidance you
were given at crucial key instances in your formative childhood years.

Through such limited perception it is possible to be living solely in
someone else's unworked-out mish-mash of a story, often comprised of
the erroneous ideologies of parents, schoolteachers and friends and have
no story to call your own. This will make you more concerned about not
making waves than walking your path and must be desisted from immediately.

To step out of that and be a hero, it is perfectly permissible and advisable to review your life, to literally see it afresh without that old set of filters and consciously create your own story from a clear uncluttered viewpoint.

Neither your story nor anyone else's, however, has more than relative value because we're all going to die one day anyway and most of the stories with us, but in the meantime, while you're here, if you can honour the game of living in stories without getting deluded by it, and achieve excellence at playing out the numerous strands of it in your own inimitable way, you *can* make loads of dosh and have a good laugh doing it till the lights go out.

If you ever find yourself locked in one of those funk-phases where you've got nothing better to do, you might experiment with making up a new version of the story of your life and set it down on paper/screen as a diagram/picture, as text, or record it as a sound file, depending on whether you're more visually, intellectually or sonically inclined.

Within the bounds of the known laws of physics and common sense, there are no limits to how grand a story you can compose [see *Compositional skills* p.170] and reasonably expect to actualise other than the following two.

The backdrop to your personal story must coincide with the known prevailing conditions for humans on Earth [see *Backdrop to the hero's adventure* p.22]. You are cast in the role of famous, fortunate hero.

This writing of the story of your life ahead of time is occurring unconsciously and continuously regardless, often according to the mangled dictates of the screwed up part of your mind, so there's nothing to lose and much fun to be had to boot in taking hold of the mechanism with full conscious awareness and shaking things up a bit.

It's the sort of thing you can do during a good daydreaming session but must be done with full knowledge that as you see it so it shall be. And precisely because you see it that way, it *will* be. And if not you can call me pisher [see *Let them call you pisher* p.101].

Writing, directing and acting out the story – and being one of the audience

(In case you get mixed up in my metaphors here, the word 'story' can be substituted by movie/play/sitcom/docudrama, etc.)

Not only do you write the story of your life as you go along, but by extension and for the full existential trip, you direct it, act it out and watch it as one of the audience too. (Physically) write down the story of your life as you see it now. For example, I live in a flat in London, I ride around town like a speed demon on a hybrid pushbike, I spend sixty hours a week working at my career and the rest of the time engaged in senseless sex with fit women.

Then do the rewrite. For example, I live in a house in the mountains, I am carried around in a sedan chair by a team of willing porters, I spend three hours a week checking up on my portfolio of international invest-ments, I write when I feel like it without thought or care for deadlines and spend forty hours a week engaging in the exploration of profound love with a woman I adore and forty-two hours imbibing high-protein drinks and pushing weights to recover.

Your story can be simple and straightforward just like this example but feel free to be elaborate if you wish. Precision is important, as this simple act of writing down has often been known 'magically' to produce the exact scenario described and the results of that are unpredictable.

To avoid trapping yourself in a future situation not to your liking when you arrive there, always add a general escape clause like, for example, there's nothing stopping me changing this situation instanta-neously, or simply, I'm always free to do what I choose in this story.

Keeping the story flexible also has a lot to do with direction as in how you interpret the script. As the director you choose the tone and atmos-phere of each scene. You do this with an awareness of lighting and angle [see *Importance of lighting and angle* p.196], in other words, as you write, you visualise the scene lit to optimum effect and shot from the most effec-tive angle to ensure the fullest possible experience of the scene both when visualising and when actually arriving at the scene in real time if it should so manifest. By practising camera angle and lighting in your visualisation you start to notice their significance more in the living theatre of daily local reality [see *Living theatre* p.40].

Just writing, visualising and directing the scene won't do the magic though. For full manifestation possibilities you have to write, see and direct yourself in the scene too. You're perfectly cast for the role. See yourself in character on set, lit right, dressed/undressed right [see *Style* p.198], doing whatever you get to do in that scene, body language how you want to see it [see *Becoming fluent in body language* p.190]. Hear the sound quality of your voice sounding kind to your ear [see *Vocal training* p.187] as you deliver the kind of chat worthy of someone of your merit, in short watch yourself acting out (both in the daydream and in real time).

Now all that's left is to make sure the audience is happy, particularly someone special out there tonight, i.e. your bold, heroic self. You are the most important personage in this august gathering and it is overwhelmingly important for you to enjoy the show. Otherwise why bother going to all this trouble putting the damn production on in the first place? If you have trouble enjoying yourself, this Handbook is intended to help you with that. *Handbook For The Urban Warrior* is also highly re-recommended [see *Marketing and cross-marketing* p.198].

Once you set the picture up it'll keep on playing itself in whichever sector of your mind has been designated for it in perpetuity. This enables you to continue to add, subtract, multiply, divide, work on props, casting, direction and so on at your whimsy as and when you choose.

This must all be done in a very light way, nothing heavy about your life story *please*. There's far too much heaviness in people's life stories these days. It's time to lighten up. The state of flux affecting life on Earth is now so strong and the outcome so totally unpredictable that there is nothing to do but drop the suffering and rejoice as there might not necessarily remain that much real-time to rejoice in.

And that's *your* job, I mean you, the hero, to lighten up and radiate that lightness for everyone. You are a hero, aren't you?

Shoot the critic

Look out there's an imposter in our midst (apart from the esteemed author)! The critic. The critic is an apparition, an hallucination, a phantasm and often a ghoul who will endeavour to self-insinuate into your consciousness posing as a bona fide punter as opposed to the parasitical waste of space he/she really is. Every time you write your life story or make any creative offering, the critic is there criticising you. And you haven't noticed yet that he/she wasn't invited. If you need constructive criticism, talk to the director. That's what he/she's being paid for. You don't need the critic, and though I'm the very last man on the planet to advocate the use of guns or any violence for that matter, I say take the fucker outside and shoot him/her. And be done with! (Now we're cookin'.)

Mechanical vs. miraculous realities

If you choose to perceive the story of your life through mechanistic, Newtonistic and rationalistic filters, I'd be forced to agree with you that, when viewed from your relatively limited perspective, the vast premise upon which the theme of this very *oeuvre* is humbly based, is simply a load of crap. So join the renunciates: put the book down and go and do something more ploddingly productive.

Or open your mind to the possibility that there is a romantic, miracle-based, quantum-physical refrain playing softly but insistently through the branches of your particular tree, that metaphysical musician being none other than your own personal muse [see *Discovering and following your Muse* p.172], whose creative power is one with *the* creative power and who guides you, protects you, sustains you and provides for you for eternity and specifically here on the local plane of your daily hero's life. *Handbook For Heroes* is only of any real use when used in concert with the romantic approach to life. How else could it be? The hero is the ultimate romantic figure. (Read on.)

Misconceptions about heroes

They never take a crap (constipated heroes – pass the laxative).
They never get scared (heroes with lobotomies).
They are always ready to die (depressive/suicidal heroes – pass the Prozac/St John's Wort).
Their motives are purely altruistic (homeless heroes – pass the hat).

They don't feel emotional or physical pain (the numb hero – pass the tweezers).
If you're not a born hero, you're not really a hero (the whingeing hero – pass that slap on the face).

Just being here, you're a hero

The real pressures of survival, though cosmetically masked by the smooth veneer of supermarket, credit card reality-simulation we fool ourselves with on a daily basis, are as immense now as they were in the caves, and soon may be more immense, who knows? And that's a pressure too – not knowing.

But you, bold being that you are, having somehow, in your own way, successfully learned to withstand these pressures, have orchestrated your affairs so elegantly that you can afford the money and precious time away from your survival duties to buy this Handbook. Respect for that – you're a hero.

And though I wax jocular, do not be fooled. I am deadly serious. As serious as the fucked-up weather patterns, the chemical weapons dumps and the teetering economies. You are a hero. Just for being here and being joined up enough in yourself to be able to make intelligible sense of the madness all around you, let alone being refined/evolved enough to make sense of this book. Now if you want to improve on that, you may find a few useful items over the course of the upcoming text.

Everyone has an inner hero waiting for the call

It could be the five minute call, as in five minutes, Mr Doctor.

It could be the call from the TV station that your programme's been accepted.

It could be the Foreign Legion.

It could be a wrong number.

Whatever the form that call arrives in, it is always essentially a call from the spirit for you to take action.

Visualising it is worthy preparational activity but unless mixed with a portion of live action, becomes mere psychic masturbation fantasy [see *Taking daily action* p.59]. What this action might be is impossible to say at this juncture, me not knowing what trip you're mixed up in, but *you'll* know when the time comes.

The call to action first emerges as an impulsion, a more or less discreet visceral urge possibly accompanied by spontaneous inner-vision, often arising repeatedly with regular frequency over a period of time. It may start out as a distant, wouldn't-it-be-nice fantasy, as in how nice it would be to pack in this night job in the bar and 'do' music full time, but increase in intensity over time to the I-must fantasy, as in I must get the fuck out of this bar and make some tunes. The call, if it is genuinely such, may then intensify until the worth of your true hero's nature is challenged.

Feel free to substitute leaving the bar and making tunes with anything heroic that springs to mind all the way up to saving the world (from itself).

To make the quantum leap from fantasy to acting out requires courage [see *Being courageous* p.54] and dedication to being a hero [see *Dedication of the hero* p.33] for the following reason:

Risky business, hero'ing

Ggggggggg go your teeth as they chatter in fear, your body trembling uncontrollably, bladder threatening to discharge its load right here, right now in the street, bowels likewise, as your adrenal glands pump in overdrive.

But you don't let it stop you. You gird those loins and walk with aplomb into the heart of the danger (the next part of your life story).

By choosing to be a hero, you're risking losing friends, lovers, family, respect, security, [see *Stepping out of your comfort zone* p.56 and *You, hero, must be prepared now to relinquish all comforts* p.58] and the ability to deceive yourself a moment longer that it's OK to go on burying your head in the sands of suburban dormitory culture (metaphorically speaking).

To pull this stunt off correctly (in whichever form it presents itself specifically to you), you must avail yourself liberally of the following heroic quality:

Confidence

Confidence derives from the Latin meaning literally holding the faith with yourself. Have faith in your choices. Have faith in your life. Have faith in your death. Have faith in your body. Have faith in your mind. Have faith in your feelings. Have faith in your spirit. And have faith in your sense of humour (because you're going to need it!). And if you say, 'I don't know how', I say you must make the following contract with yourself, hero:

'I agree with all my heart, soul, and mind to have faith in myself from now on for the rest of my life. I back this agreement up with my life.'

Loneliness of the hero

I mean, look at me now. In a room. On my own. Photek playing on the hi-fi at a discreet level, halogen light burning elegantly over my keyboard. My new top-of-the-range chair supporting me nicely as I tip-tap away at the keys fantasising about voice recognition programs and this beautiful Persian queen of a woman I know, in between splurges of creative outpouring.

Not many people know I'm in town. When I'm writing, I let it be known I'm off the planet for that time and people assume I'm away. Otherwise the phone doesn't stop ringing with heavy attentional demands as you'd expect with a healer-hero such as myself. (I'm not complaining.) But then I can't concentrate myself into the correct shape to write.

So here I sit, as ever poised at the edge of a freefall waffle tumble, I've taken the critic outside and shot him at least eight times today, my fingers keep itching to turn on the phone and call someone. 'Do you care I exist?' I'll ask to save time so I can make it quick and get back to the writing.

And it's not just the necessary creative confinements the hero must undergo that can engender loneliness.

Ojas, the natural-born hero who sleeps rough on a Himalayan mountainside with the wild monkeys, bears and leopards as company and who comes down to the village once a day to teach Tai Chi, he gets lonely from time to time out there with the bugs and stuff.

Jamie-The-Famous-Pop-Star (JTFPS) playing gigs in front of fifty-five thousand fans, his single coming in at No. 2 in Germany this week, No. 1 in Holland, No. 4 in the UK, and set to start a year-long world tour in a blaze of electronic glory – he gets lonely on the road.

The choices you make as a hero you make alone. The consequences of those choices are your own. And that gets lonely for you sometimes. Thing is, everyone's in the same boat whether they realise it or not.

The up-side of the hero's lonely patches is that it's during these times that your Muse talks to you loudest, if you're open to it. If you say, 'I don't know how to do that', I say, make the following contract with your self:

'*I agree to open myself to creative input originating from my Muse or from any point of origin with a good smell to it. I agree to be especially susceptible to creative input during lonely patches.*'

You want to be a hero, you've got to be strong, new-ageisms aside. Loneliness is only loneliness. (Pass the phone.)

The opposite to this state is overload where the demand for your presence and services is temporarily so great that you need to clone yourself five times over just to handle all the phone calls [see *Telephone technique* p.189]. This, however, is not the antidote to loneliness, which can be found in practising the art of introspection [see *Meditation* p.126].

Dedication of the hero

Your first dedication is to the path (Tao) and you include all other dedications in that (lovers, family, friends, addictions and so on).

If you say, 'I don't know what you're talking about', I say, make the following declaration out loud with your hand on your heart in the presence of a reliable witness, next time you're drunk or stoned, or are feeling naturally weird:

'I do declare [in Southern Belle accent] *I dedicate my life to following my path as a hero and am willing to take on all associated responsibilities whatever they may turn out to be.*'

Reliable witness then states, 'Well, I declare!' and the ceremony's over.

The way dedication shows up is in the following vital quality:

Persistence of the hero

Through rain and hail, sleet and slurry, rejection and humiliation, despondency and defeat, you've just got to keep going. That's all there is to it. Persistence requires the minimum amount of energy expenditure, like keeping the soup on simmer.

Persistence is entirely different from obsession which requires maximum energy expenditure and is like having the flame on full for two hours and forgetting to put the soup on the hob.

Persistence requires only a gentle sticking to the plot with no more than a metaphysical four ounces of pressure.

The hero does everything with grace (except when being a prat/geek).

Willingness to sacrifice all for the quest

Family, friends, comfort, lifestyle, security, possibly your sanity, status, respect, home, cosiness, and possibly privacy and anonymity are all things you may have to give up in the quest and, in any case, have to leave at the door when you die, so what the hell. You willing to do that?

If not, maybe you can discover another way to find meaning in your life. Many others have. The hero's is not the only path.

Or perhaps you're only willing to go halfway. I've never heard of half-a-hero, but I don't see any reason you shouldn't have a go.

If you feel you're willing to let go of everything you hold dear, if needs be, to follow your path, you'll experience a massive influx of personal power by stating:

'I'm willing to let go of everything I hold dear, if needs be, to follow my path as a hero.'

And, if you play your cards right, you may never have the loss.

I told you you must be mad wanting to be a hero.

In practice, it is often extremely difficult emotionally to contemplate letting go of those and that which you love and no hero except for the most psychopathically deranged can expect to maintain this level of detached compassion without the occasional wobble.

You can *never* fulfil your potential

Your potential is limitless. How can it be fulfilled? Though when I say limitless, it is actually limited by your own beliefs. Which is why it is so important to examine your beliefs about yourself.

This doesn't mean you shouldn't have a good pop at it though. It's this unrequited urge which has engendered our 'progress' on the planet. Without it we would have no high achievers, probably no wheel and subsequent technology, no impending ecological disaster (maybe), and we'd still be threatening each other with clubs instead of missiles.

It's the basic urge to excel but as perfect limitless potential fulfilment is an unachievable paradox, don't let your pursual of it make you lose perspective. Remember, a hero is allowed to fall short. It's OK, no one's really keeping score, no one that counts anyway, you're not being record-ed at this moment (I assume) so relax.

Being your own hero

The point is you probably think being a hero is all about being a hero in someone else's eyes, your girl/boyfriend, mother/father, the general public, etc. but what's the point of that? You can never enjoy it!

No, my bold friend, firstly and foremost you must be a hero in your own eyes. Be your own hero above all other heroes, no matter how great they appear to you, nor how lowly you appear to you. Above *all* else, be your own hero. I mean, whose story is this anyway? Why pay good money to watch someone else have all the fun?

Being other people's hero

Becoming someone else's hero is none of your business. It's theirs, exclu-sively. Obviously being adopted as a hero figure for someone is a great honour but should not be taken seriously. Today's hero is often tomor-row's anti-hero and vice versa.

When someone else adopts you as a hero figure, they are merely pro-jecting their own latent hero nature on to their image of you. That's their process entirely and has nothing to do with you yourself.

When you find yourself in this position, do not therefore take it per-sonally. Instead use it, if you must use it at all, to inspire those to whom you are held as an object of hero-worship, to discover and develop their own heroic qualities (exactly as I am doing now).

Never get stuck on needing other people's hero-worship or you'll soon turn into a dried-up fossil.

So when other people call you hero and appear to worship you in that way, simply wish them the clarity, perspective, imagination and courage to be their own hero. Doing so does not in any way diminish you as a hero, neither in standing nor essence, and will, in fact, increase you in both.

The important part of being a hero, the valuable part, happens in private, often completely unwitnessed other than by your own inner witness/audience, director/higher self and any other straggler from the spiritual realms who's got nothing better to do than float about watching you perform all day.

The hero's pain

The pain of the hero is the pain of the whole world (poor sod!).

You feel the world's pain. That's why you're so keen to save the world from suffering. That's what makes you a hero, *and* mad! Admirable but mad.

The world can never be saved from its pain. Without pain, there would be no striving to improve life. There would be no growth. (There would be no bondage clubs.) Torturers would go out of business. Armies would be obsolete and everyone would be happy and smiling the long day through. Suburban paradise.

Well, it's not going to happen. You'll never put an end to pain. Yours or the world's. So you have to learn to sit with it. To feel it but not let it stop or obstruct you. Like when you've got a period but you're wearing new ultra-whatevers so you can still play tennis.

You'll never put a stop to pain, hero, but you can help by jollying up yourself and others in the midst of it.

Other than the existential pain of life, both personal and universal, the hero is prone to all the same mundane aches and pains as the non-hero, from which ibuprofen, codeine and other standard painkillers will usually supply adequate relief if alternative methods are unavailable or impractical [see *Self-healing* p.168].

The key to managing/diminishing pain, of whichever nature, is to breathe out firmly and resolutely into it and to desist from holding your breath against it [see *Fundamentals: Breathing* p.128]. For example, if you have an ache in the left side of your brain, exhale imagining the breath shooting into the pain spot and acting as a healing agent to disperse the pain.

If the pain is emotional it will automatically translate itself into physical pain or tension somewhere in your body, usually in your solar plexus (upper-abdominal) region. By breathing out into the physical tension you will simultaneously disperse the emotional upset.

But don't get stuck dwelling on the pain, focus your attentions instead on the following:

The hero's pleasure

This arises from:

Satisfaction of saving/rescuing people from danger, injustice and oppression.

Satisfaction of getting the girl/boy.

Satisfaction of being satisfied if you don't get the girl/boy.

Pleasant stimulation of your sense organs by various means, just like anyone else.

Remembering that you're free to do whatever you choose.

Choosing wisely [see *Making decisions – pendulums, Tarot, I Ching* p.61].

Experiencing moments of pure excellence in your actions.

Completing challenging projects or tasks.

Getting the cheque in and paying it into your bank.

The most effective way to manage/increase pleasure, whether physical or emotional, is the same as with pain; breathe out firmly into it. Imagine your breath is a healing agent which magnifies, expands and amplifies your sensation of pleasure.

With enough breathing you may notice both pleasure and pain, just like fame and ignomy, or fortune and impoverishment, are merely opinions. Never take your opinions (or those of others) too seriously.

Combining all-too-human with super-human

Being a hero and channelling that by becoming master/mistress of the Five Excellences [see *Impossibility of mastery* p.116], especially the first three, meditation, martial arts and healing, will certainly lend you super-human powers. Of that there is no doubt.

What it won't do is delete the all-too-human aspects of your menta and behavioural repertoire.

Avarice, vanity, greed, anxiety, resentment, jealousy, meanness, treach erousness, deceitfulness, dishonesty, cowardice, flakiness, vanity, pride lust, foolishness, stupidity, narrow-mindedness, laziness, prejudice confusion, muddle-headedness, impatience, addictiveness, insecurity an any other human 'failing' you care to add, will always be part of you psyche, no matter how much of a hero you are (or become).

To deny their existence is to split off part of your psyche. That spli away part, in fact, then goes underground, deep into the unexplore regions of your unconscious mind, and will surface at a later stage, ofte at wholly inappropriate times, magnified in ferocity like a wild anim escaping from a cage.

To sort out this conundrum can take years and cost you a fortune i psychotherapy bills, so it could work out a lot cheaper in the long run t accept the above list with any additions you care to make, as constitutin the dark, too-human part of yourself. Like you have a higher self, yo also have a lower self. It is essential to have a lower self. Without it you higher self would fall over.

But what to do about it?

Not much. Simply watch. Watch and breathe. That'll ground you.

As Russell-The-Spiritual-Firefighter (RTSFF), hero of genuine real-lif merit, ex-fireman, saver of lives, now spiritually enlightened and war dering the globe's trouble spots, setting up soup kitchens for th homeless and healing people, including kids who've just been stabbec *and* making a tip-top TV documentary of his adventures as he goes, say 'I love it when I get fucked up because it grounds me.'

All you have to do to be like Russell (in this respect) is say to yoursel 'Ah, there's me being greedy/anxious/lustful/resentful/jealous/whateve again!'

Don't judge yourself guilty for it though. Just breathe, observe an accept. Accepting, though, doesn't mean giving yourself permission t act out the dark urge. You *can* do that if you want, but people may suffe and there will be consequences of a correspondingly dark nature whic may cause you indigestion or something worse.

It is precisely this ability to observe serenely, compassionately your too-human urges, that affords you the time and clarity to choose how you want to use the dark force. Positively or negatively.

Containment of a dark urge, through breathing and self-observation [see *Meditation* p.126] will sublimate its power and transform it in a trice into something more positive and socially useful. You may try talking a problem out with somebody, calmly and respectfully instead of smacking them on the side of the head, for instance. Then again you may not.

This game's about developing a myth that has existed since you were old enough to think

To manage the vast amount of information assailing you at around the time of moment one, post womb, you constructed a self. The 'You' who did the construction work is real/eternal. The self you constructed is not. It's merely relative/local, as it only exists in relation to your environment; it only arose as a response to your environment.

Real self equals hero.

Relative self equals the art form you have created for yourself. It's a myth. First you started believing it, then others did too. And why not, it's perfectly fine myth. It didn't prevent you from getting here at this point in time. Maybe it could use a bit of polishing, maybe some filing down or bit of padding out, that's up to you (if you want to get finickity). But I say take the myth you've got, the art form you've developed of yourself, the self you've constructed and say 'Here I am!' Proclaim it loud and proclaim it proud, because nobody on the face of this Earth can prove you wrong on that.

You who constructed yourself are not a myth. You simply watch and regenerate the myth, breathing in, breathing out. Simply watch and regenerate. And you can develop the myth as you see fit. In the same way you can develop muscles by training weights without altering the fundamental structure of your body, you can also develop your constructed self along desirable lines without fundamentally altering the structure of your timeless true self [see *The Five Excellences* p.121].

So why bother? you may ask.

To make something of yourself in this world!

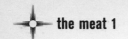

Just like everyone else. Everyone is perpetrating a myth about them selves. Everyone else plays the game of believing it. The president gets his dick sucked, allegedly. (The president has a dick.) The president tells porkie pies. Shock horror! It's all a charade. We're all playing. There is no other game in town. Playing does not make you insincere. Sincerity quotas are entirely at your discretion. You can play like an asshole or you can play like a hero. The whole prawn is one big piece of living theatre.

Living theatre

Every line uttered, every swirl of a skirt, every turn of an ankle, every shout, groan, scream, laugh, every social, business, emotional, sexual, physical, militaristic, political or spiritual encounter, and every storyline and dramatic development is all just the acting out of living theatre (Shiva's Dance).

Knowing this helps you not to take it personally if things don't work out the way you anticipated.

Your anticipation is an event in itself which may or may not coincide with the way things show up in real-time. You're merely the actor/audience member so don't get your knickers in a metaphysical twist over it. Just say to yourself, 'It's all just living theatre', over and over like a mantra, as you wander down the boulevard of broken dreams.

The living theatre comprises all the personal life-story dramas of every individual on the planet [see *Fictionalising your life* p.25], which is why collectively, we manifest such a conundrum.

All the plot lines are pre-set. Likewise all the available roles.

The plot and the parts will be acted out on the stage of living theatre regardless of the actors involved. For each scene, someone has to play the bad guy, someone the good. Sometimes you'll be one, sometimes the other. And if you can't make it for that day's shoot, on account of death or other such contingencies, someone else will be there to take the part. Don't take it personally (but the show must go on!).

Being a star

You can either be a star, a black hole, a planet, moon, asteroid, comet, meteor, or empty space.

Of these, stars are best. If you're a star you're always shining, always hot, and in control of most of what goes on around you.

If you're a black hole you have to reside in the dangerous realms of anti-matter which is known to cause bad breath and make it hard to find friends, not to mention suitable partners.

If you're a planet you stand the risk of getting loads of little people crawling all over your surface, irritating your skin and bringing you out in a rash.

If you're a moon, you get spaceships landing on your head and otherwise it's dead boring.

If you're an asteroid the only action you get is the occasional errant little runt of a prince, and if you're a comet you go past too quickly for anyone to celebrate and that makes people nervous and blame you for all their calamities.

If you're a meteor you're too small to worry about.

If you're empty space you're too big and amorphous. No one would know how to hang a story on you, you'd be difficult to package and market and you're forever hanging around providing the context for everyone else to skip about in and have fun.

So be a star.

Everything is held in orbit by the gravitational pull of the star. You may enjoy experiencing the thrill of seeing your planet, moon, asteroid, meteor and comet friends spinning merrily and variously in orbit around you at the party. But always allow others to be stars too, otherwise you become a black hole that swallows everyone up and then you'll have no friends to play with. Remember it's a big galaxy we're cavorting in. After the party you can go home and be empty space [see *Meditation* p.126] to refresh yourself for the next round.

You don't need to be seen stepping out of a stretch limo to be a star. You don't need to be seen wiggling your two first fingers and thumb in the air to signal you want to pay the overpriced bill in a fancy restaurant.

You don't even need to have the details of your personal life distorted and twisted out of recognisable shape and then be broadcast publicly to satisfy the purient interests of sad fucks with nothing better to do with their time, just so someone can sell a few newspapers.

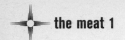

All you have to do is say, aloud or a'quiet, 'I am a star!'

Then for eight whole days treat yourself as a star. If you don't have much money to play with yet, treat yourself as a star who's left his/her wallet (US pocketbook) at home and is studying form for a new role as someone who doesn't have much money yet, by living it, method acting style.

Remember the sun doesn't have to *do* anything to be a star except shine, and nor do you.

And you don't have to be a pompous star. You can be a naturally modest, gracefully humble star. But be a star. This is your movie. Why be anything less?

If you were an editor, would you suggest this item is redundantly repeating the substance of previous items and recommend its immediate removal? No. Because it's sheer poetry! (Nonsense in places, perhaps, but poetry none the less.)

Shining

When you shine, you shine and when you don't, you don't. It's a basic law of universal nature. You can't force yourself to shine. People try with cocaine [see *Cocaine as a social/personality stimulant* p.111], but the effects are very short-term and before long you're just spouting overexcitable nonsense.

Shining is not a surface phenomenon. You shine when your inner light is strong and your body, face and especially eyes are relaxed and energised enough to facilitate a clear conduit for the light to reach the surface and radiate out.

Visualise the sun burning brilliant in the centre of your chest for no more than one minute, forty seconds at a time, over the course of thirty-six hours, or until it's clearly visible to your inner eye at all times. Once it's holding steady on its own, your lowest shine level will be increased to a satisfactory enough degree to sustain a sparkle even at your most lacklustre. If this doesn't work, simply go home and have an early night.

The mystery of charisma

When your inner light is strong, confidence steady, mind clear and energy flow unimpeded, your aura (external energy field) takes on an intense golden hue, visible to the trained eye, known popularly as charisma.

Charisma acts like a magnet drawing people's attention towards you, which adds to your charisma and so sets up an increasing charisma spiral (ICS). People with high degrees of fame have especially high levels of ICS.

Charisma can be activated and enhanced by visualisation methods [see *Hardcore practice: Secret (no longer) Taoist energy control and visualisation mechanism for generating charisma* p.135].

The name of the game is fame or shame

Once you put you and/or your product out into the market place to join the general affray, if you want to sell units, whether it's buttocks on seats, CDs spinning, perfume behind ears or books in hands (Handbooks), in sufficient numbers, your profile or your product's profile must be 'high' enough to stimulate demand.

Degrees of profile height equate to degrees of fame [see *Degrees of fame and fortune* p.73]. Hence, if you don't achieve enough degrees of fame, your product sticks and that's a shame. Of course you can always come back later with a new angle, repackaged product or entirely new product [see *Persistence of the hero* p.33].

Taking on fame to any degree requires boldness, self-acceptance and self-esteem in adequate amounts to allow you to risk exposing yourself. There is no place for shame in this equation. Take shame outside with the critic next time you go and shoot its brains out. No need to indulge in it a moment longer. Accept all of yourself, however bad and disgusting some parts of you may be, and bring it all together to the market place as one unified whole.

There is nothing so reassuring as being around someone who accepts the worst in themselves, because it means they accept you too, which helps you accept yourself, and everyone loves that. Self-acceptance will increase your popularity in proportion to the degree you accept yourself.

Popularity leads to fame. So if you want to be famous, accept yourself as you are and bear it proudly to market.

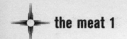

Idealised media-inspired image of the hero vs. the real hero

Of course it would be wild to have the 'perfect' body, ideally symmetrical facial features, just the right height, and be graced with all the fine personal qualities a hero should have, including unfailing courage, unwavering faith and resolve, integrity and valour, nobility and honesty, natural modesty and a constantly calm and cheerful disposition, and if you have, good luck to you.

But let's get real. No one has.

I'm certainly not and it doesn't stop me being a hero. There's no reason it should stop you either. There's something incredibly heroic about the twenty-one-year-old girl with two amputated lower legs, who has taught herself to walk on false ones, refuses to use a wheelchair, holds down a responsible, well-paid job, has a happy relationship with an able-bodied man, and is never heard to complain.

So don't be discouraged if your self-image doesn't match up to the ideal media image of the hero. Every hero is a unique art form. Honour that.

Doing it with conviction

No matter what the part you're playing in the drama, play it with conviction. Even if it's complete crap, do it with conviction and you'll probably get away with it. Remember it's all a big con game. Confidence – conviction, it's all the same thing.

Don't shy away from your part even if it's temporarily a weak one. Play it with conviction and in time you'll turn it into a strong one.

Of course, it helps dramatically if there's some substance to what you have to offer, at which point it becomes twice as important to offer it with conviction. Doing it with conviction does not necessitate being extrovert, however. You can be that if it's working, but you can also be an introverted moody bastard and get away with it.

You ever watch a real hero? A hero working in the relatively humble job of serving behind the counter at the coffee bar. She's such a star, playing the role with such conviction, good humour and grace that the place is transformed into a palace and she's the queen and people, especially men, come from miles around just to pick up a simple sandwich.

Watch 360 minutes of prime-time TV, not including movies, over the course of a week, looking out for conviction levels in the players/performers/presenters. Only perform this highly dangerous feat once, for apart from the excessive level of gamma-rays you may be exposing yourself to, your mind is in danger of turning to mulch.

The hero's path (Tao)

Where are all the heroes? On the hero's path. The further you travel down your own hero's path, the more you start to notice them all around you. You'll find them in all walks of life. There are no age, gender, status, wealth, race, or religion barriers to heroism.

Most heroes are incognito. Could be the check-out girl who's doing a PhD, nursing her sick mother and dancing competition tango (it could?!). Could be the bouncer who's saving enough money to visit Timbuktu and explore the Dogon tribe's knowledge of Sirius. Could be the eighty-five-year-old doctor who devotes her failing energy to caring for an under-privileged community in the roughest part of town. You don't often get to see the hero in people until you see it in yourself and know the signs to look for, and then you see them everywhere. (Try it for yourself.)

But this is mostly immaterial to you except for when you need a bit of inspiration or heroic company, because you're focused on your own path.

Your path is your Tao, your own personal Great Thoroughfare through the living theatre. No one knows how it got there. Perhaps it arose of itself. Or perhaps your spirit/higher self/true self laid it out sometime back in the sands of eternity. But no matter how it arose, the life story you write for yourself will be acted out along this path.

Other than to the physical reality of death, no one knows where the path leads. Maybe to the grail, maybe to oblivion. But the onward pull is irresistible and there must be something good waiting for us because everyone seems to be going that way and no one ever seems to come back.

Establish a good, loving relationship with your path. I mean, right now, stop for a moment and visualise your path. I hope it looks welcoming. If not, change it (in your imagination). Now surrender to it. Give it your trust. Talk to it just like you would any road upon which you're about to set out on a thousand-mile hike. Say, 'Dear path, thank you for devoting your existence to facilitating my journey. I hereby release all my anxiety and doubt, and surrender myself to your pull, in full trust and faith that you're leading me somewhere good.'

Now, if you're quite finished talking to imaginary paths, let your mind be still and your breathing tranquil so you can be receptive to the path-ward (wayward) urge.

The path reveals itself in following your fascination

Whatever fascinates you, follow it. Fascination, deriving from the Latin *fascinare*, means having a spell put on or bewitching you. When an idea puts a spell on you and pulls you in a certain direction with enough intensity and persistence, you follow it. It's that simple. It's not a question of morals. Obviously, if your fascinations are dark and bad for health, the path will lead you that way to teach you whatever you need to know. But if your fascinations are light and life-affirming, your path will lead you that way to get your lessons. Doesn't matter which way you choose because you're going to die either way. It's just that if you follow the latter, you'll enjoy the journey more and help others likewise. The other way you cause more suffering. But, like I say, it doesn't really matter. Someone's got to play the bad guy [see *Living theatre* p.40].

But let's say your fascination is for beautiful tunes. So you follow the fascination. You buy the tunes, read magazines, maybe meet someone with recording facilities who invites you to watch how they make tunes. Maybe they like you so much they let you twiddle a knob or two. Maybe, before you know it, you've made a tune and your tune gets on a late-night radio show. Maybe the DJ invites you on to talk about the tune and you get to talking about all the tunes you like. Maybe the producer likes your person-ality and invites you to DJ on your own show. Maybe now you're the most famous DJ in the land [see *Importance of PR (perception management)* p.200]. And during the interview for the Saturday papers to talk about the new CD you've got coming out, they ask you if you always wanted to be the most famous DJ in the land, and you answer that you always had a fascination for a good tune and the path just seemed to lead you this way.

Or maybe your fascination's with sex, but I'm not going to talk that one through, save to say the following:

It's gotsta be sexy

This is a recurring Barefoot Doctor's Handbook theme. If you're going to take the trouble to walk the hero's path, make it sexy. Do not imagine that the path is more respectful to you if you walk down it like a sexless frump [see *Style* p.197].

Everyone does sexy in a different way and I don't presume to advise you on that. Of course it's got something to do with smell, on a subtle level at least. You've got to like your own smell. You are perfectly at liberty to enhance it by mixing it with sensual or even saucy scents.

It's also in the way you walk. Your hips and buttocks have to be relaxed and proud to house those beautiful sexual organs of yours.

Of course, you have to love your genitals, not obsessively, but proudly and joyfully. Proclaim out loud from the rooftops, 'I love my sexual organs!' Actually – nice image, but perhaps better if you say it to yourself or, better still, say it to your genitals. The last thing you need, if you want to be sexy, is for your genitals to feel they're being left out in the cold. So it never harms to reassure them from time to time.

That's fundamental, baby-level stuff but is, in fact, pretty much at the core of most sexual problems.

You're sexy when you take command.
You're sexy when you display confidence, conviction, courage and dedication; in short, the qualities of the hero.
Being a hero makes you sexy. You don't even have to do anything about it, just be aware, and say, 'God, I'm sexy!'
Breathing in and out of your sexual organs as if you had a nose there (your own) helps to intensify your sexiness.
When you're in tune with your sexuality, everything you do will be sexy, your creative outpourings, your career moves, your bicycle riding, your copulating, everything.

This will make you and your product more desirable. It's not naughty to

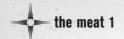

be sexy. It can be if you want it to be, if you need the forbidden fruit stimulus, but intrinsically it's not naughty. Sexiness is feeling the erotic quality in everything that transpires. Eroticism comes from Eros. Eros was a god. Hence, eroticism is spiritual, so how can it be naughty?

But there's no point just going around being sexy all day. There's something else you need to make the story hang together.

Having a message to deliver to the world

Every hero has a message for the world. The message itself, though arising from the very origins of consciousness (the Tao), is never original. There's nothing you can say that hasn't in essence been said at least two hundred and thirty thousand times before. What you do that is original is to frame that message in a unique context, i.e. your unique expression [see *Compositional skills* p.170 and *Presentation skills* p.180].

When formulating your message to the world, do not be intimidated if it at first appears obscured by complexity. Go to the essence, the root of what you want for the world. It's always something simple and straightforward, like the following examples:

ease off
lighten up
stop struggling
everything is relative (Lao Tsu/Einstein)
know joy
you're free
have a laugh
appreciate what you've got (before it's too late)
existence is a miracle
you are a spiritual being
you can do miracles
everything is connected
there are no limits to what we can accomplish together
love is the fuel

Take some time drawing your message down from the ether, or up from your unconscious mind whichever you're in the mood for [see *Discovering and following your Muse* p.172]. Ask for it to be revealed in your dreams, or as signs in your waking hours. Then pay attention, be receptive and, sure as the next procrastination break I'm going to take, the message will come. It's what you'd say if you had the whole world gathered before you and you were allowed to make one utterance and one utterance only. This is an utterance from the heart, an utterance of true passion/compassion. That's how you can verify its authenticity.

Once you've got your message, you can really have fun because now you've got a purpose, and a purpose is one of the most valuable treasures in the world. Purpose gives you a self-impelling reason to be on the path.

Pissing in the wind

So you dedicate your whole life to putting out your message of peace and love and you look around you, or more specifically at the TV news or newspaper page, and you can't help feeling like you're pissing in the wind.

With every sign of ascending light, you get a sign of ascending darkness to match it. And it doesn't really matter. You're having such a laugh doing it, and you can't think of anything better to do with your time.

But you'll never fully or even partly know the effect your life is having on the world. The healer doesn't get to watch the patient's healing process. That happens after the healing session in the patient's own time.

So carry on pissing!

Having front

In order to get away with this heroic stunt of putting out your message to the world, thus risking opprobrium and ridicule, you need buckets of the above.

But there's no point having front if you haven't got back. Without adequate back, your front will eventually slide off your body and on to the floor in a pile of insubstantial egoplasm. So if you want to develop a strong front, develop a strong back to support it [see *Martial arts* p.138].

There are two aspects to back development, the external and the internal. The external aspect is obvious: weights, push-ups, pull-ups, yogic backbends, cobras, headstands, handstands, swimming, martial arts training and tango dancing are only some examples.

The importance of regular, consistent, intelligently and sensitively performed back-strengthening exercise can not possibly be overstated. The internal aspect is so elementary-dear-Watson, it almost doesn't qualify as a fully fledged aspect and comprises merely being aware of your back at all times. Most of the time you're only aware of your front, because your internal organs and genitals are there, your eyes are there, your nose is there, your ears are inclined to listen in front, your mouth is there, and when you speak, the sound goes out in front of you.

So it's not often you remember your back unless it's hurting. And what way is that to treat such a staunch friend and ally? Someone who's carried you through your whole life so far and is committed to carry on carrying you until you die, all things being equal.

Perhaps it's worthy of a little more respect than you've been showing. A little more attention. So become aware of your back at all times and do what you can to strengthen it on a daily basis. This will allow your front to relax more and, when you're relaxed, you perform better. Put another way, when you experience being physically well supported by your back, you'll feel more self-secure and thus more able to use your front effectively.

Train your ears to listen behind you as well as in front.

Being original

Be original in the way you express yourself. Copy people only long enough to discover your own style of doing what they do that you admire. But don't plagiarise or do second-rate, supermarket-music-style versions of other people's superior work. There are enough people doing that, but they're not heroes, so take no notice. You have to be original, as in connected to the origins of creativity [see *The significance of developing a creative channel* p.52], or you're not a hero, you're a ponce.

Knowing who your audience is

So here you are, tripping merrily down the path, full of message and ready to spout, but who are you going to give it to?

Anyone who'll listen. Don't be proud. Start with one. Then two. If you get two, you're doing well.

Two people agreeing wholeheartedly with you gives you enough psycho-emotional clout to start the process of quantum-leaping your appeal to a wider target audience.

In order to reach everyone, i.e. the mainstream, you have to keep quantum-leaping. Start with those people/friends who relate most easily to the context in which you're putting the message across, i.e. your expression. Once you have adequate support, take it public.

Target sensibly. A snow/skateboarding clothing range goes to a hip-hop/drum'n'bass market, etc. This requires research, as in talking to people [see *Importance of networking* p.109]. Establish a fan-base of loyal customers among your specialist target audience. Once having established a relatively stable floating platform, your product, i.e. you, if it has enough integral value and social relevance, is poised exponentially to expand its spread into the wider mainstream market.

Targetting yourself at a specialist group is facilitated by modern communication systems such as digital/cable TV, Internet channels, etc., themselves dedicated by dint of their sheer numbers to reaching specialist target audiences.

It also allows more for bold/subtle acts of cultural terrorism. You can take chances, push the envelope of respectability [see *Being outrageous* p.55], and derive great creative satisfaction and amusement as you watch agreement levels reach critical mass point and your product erupt into the wide open market.

Anything new that's good starts off as an underground bubbling long before it gathers enough force to come up overground into the harsh and often ugly light of mainstream tabloid reality.

The longer the gestation period, the better as this allows you to develop the psychic strength necessary to withstand public acclaim overload (PAO) if it should occur. There's no age limit to entering the hero game, so be patient and persistent and allow yourself to cook properly before risking premature PAO.

You don't want to peak too soon, creatively or otherwise. It makes you bloated. Nor must you overcook yourself, i.e. hide your light under a bushel so long it fizzles out [see *Taking risks daily* p.60].

In other words, don't rush to the mainstream. Bide your time persistently, developing a meaningful dialogue with the audience you have and, in time, if your product merits it [see *Dealing with fear of rejection/humiliation* p.100] the mainstream will come rushing to you [see *Opening bank accounts as receptacles* p.208].

The significance of developing a creative channel

Without a creativity channel, your unique message to the world will have no expression. It may float around unformed and shapeless in the murky depths of your unconscious for the rest of your life and never see the light of day. To grab the message and give it formation (shape) in your conscious mind transforms it literally into information (in formation), which can, once you've crafted it, be used by others to their advantage and thus entitle you to the benefits of f'n'f, to the degree that you are able successfully to package that information into acquirable units and sell them in sufficient quantities to cause a stir.

The information you offer may be in the form of a service, like healing for example, in which case the units you're selling are units of time.

Your information may be in the form of a live or filmed performance, which people pay to watch, in which case the units you're selling are tickets at the door.

If your information is in the form of a clothing range, you're selling units of (yes) clothing.

If you're working in a straightforward job, the units of information you're selling consist of your time, energy, attention and obedience [see below, *The significance of being your own boss*].

Whatever the units you're selling, the more creatively you channel the information of which those units are comprised, the more you get paid per unit. That makes sense, doesn't it?

Once you've found your creativity you can apply it to anything and everything.

The significance of being your own boss

I am aware that if enough people follow this path, there would be economic and social anarchy. Nice problem to have.

Advantages of being the boss (of self or others)

Within the legal and infrastructurally defined parameters laid down and enforced in the land in which you operate, you are free to do whatever you choose, specifically with regard to getting your message out to the world.

You determine your own timetable. Not just on a daily basis, but weekly, monthly, yearly or tri-annually if you want.

You can devote most of your waking time to developing, materialising, promoting and marketing your idea.

You determine your own goals and intentions and owe obedience to no one except your muse perhaps [see *Discovering and following your Muse* p.172].

You have the more or less constant thrill of living on the financial edge [*see Gambling* p.210].

You have complete autonomy over all decision-making.

You can work wherever you choose. (Its true electronic communication systems are triggering a trend towards self-empowerment/working at home, making autonomy over choice of workplace more common among employees in large companies as well, but let's not humour each other, you're still tied.)

You can work however you choose (say you like to be naked in a headstand talking on the phone, for example).

Disadvantages of working for someone else

If you like to be slave to someone else's system (idea).

If you like to devote most of your waking hours to promoting someone else's message and have no time to promote your own, let alone go out for a walk when you feel like it without having to make an excuse.

If you like to hand your power over to other people and let them make your decisions for you.

If you have no basic trust in the providence of the universe, and potentially unstable cash-flow situations make you anxious.

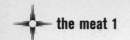

If you like travelling in traffic jams/overstuffed public transport facilities twice a day just to be a player in someone else's theatre (remember this is your life!).

Then there are no disadvantages.

But don't rush to give up your day job

If you've got your message and you're working towards packaging it and it's currently financially expedient for you to support yourself by working at a day job (this could be anything from waiting tables to managing a bank), then you must play the role to the full [see *Living theatre* p.40].

By playing your role with full conviction, the good energy you spread about you will eventually come back and whoosh you out of there to concentrate on your own thing as soon as you're ready.

If you're working in a bar, that becomes your art form and you do it with excellence. You're honouring your own life like this and by extension all life and in so doing will attract life opportunities to you. The man ordering a cappuccino will turn out to be the facilitator of your next commercial carry-on or whatever.

But don't lose your sense of proportion about things. Playing the day job role with conviction does not mean sacrificing your own plot and storyline. If you've got an important meeting/shoot/session, etc. in connection with getting your message out, you do it.

And if that seriously conflicts with your day-job boss's agenda and you have to leave the day job, you leave the day job [see *Just say 'fuck 'em!'* p.104]

Being courageous

Courage is a quality of an open heart, not as in surgery, but as in relaxing your chest. Relax your chest now, as you read. You may become aware of a point exactly in the middle of your breastbone. This is your heart centre or 'crimson place', your personal psychic-energy fountain of courage (from the Old French, *corage*, from Latin *cor* meaning heart).

You need courage to get out of bed in the morning. You need courage to propel yourself through the day. It's this same courage you need to propel yourself to the dizzio-glitzy heights of fame and fortune.

Having courage does not preclude having fear.

Displaying courage does not preclude displaying vulnerability, in fact displaying courage with vulnerability is becoming highly fashionable.

Witnessing a display of vulnerable human courage is one of the most moving experiences in life.

Make as much use of courage as you can. The more you use it, the stronger it gets. Start every day with the knowledge that you have the courage to optimise on every opportunity that comes your way.

Kabbalists visualise the Archangel Michael standing to their right, as huge as the universe, pumping them with courage. They don't have a patent out on it, so feel free to avail yourself.

Wayward Taoists, while quite likely to 'borrow' such techniques from time to time, are usually more inclined simply to breathe in and out of the central point in the chest as if they had a breathing aperture such as a nose or a mouth situated there. With every breath they take in and out 'through' their breastbone, they visualise/feel courage expanding in their chest. (Try this for yourself.)

Being outrageous

You have to be careful with this [see *Style* p.197]. Society, Western at least, broke through the cultural outrage barrier during the latter part of the second half of the 1900s, and there is nothing cultural I can think of, however ugly, disgusting, vile or nasty, that falls within the bounds of legality that would actually shock the so-called public, i.e you and me, into a state of outrage.

Of course, I accept that I only enjoy a limited viewpoint upon which to base this assumption, but so inured are we, it would seem, by over-exposure to artistic envelope pushing, that if you want to exercise your right to outrage, which I strongly recommend you do in the pursuit of getting your message across, exercise it with restraint.

In a cultural atmosphere of outrageousness-overload, *outrageousness is only effective if it's subtle.* You can no longer bang people on the head with your outrageousness and expect to get a result. People's heads are too used to it. A persistent whisper among the shouts will eventually have far more effect than a short-lived burst of a scream.

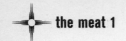

Speak your truth!

That's outrageous enough in itself. It's just a matter of learning to contain your outrageousness within a context relevant to your milieu. To be outrageous effectively, your outrageousness has to rest on something substantial. Your message must be authentic, i.e. it must be your truth.

I can't tell you how to be outrageous. It's all relative. The late Frank E Kramer, one of the greatest, most outrageous psychotherapists and phil anthropists of the late twentieth century, used to paint his little toenai red, sometimes wear a woman's permed wig over his shaved-bald hea and keep a completely straight face when sitting with a patient or whe in a business meeting to discuss his various, not inconsiderable invest ments. If anyone asked him why, which interestingly happened rarely he'd reply simply, 'To remind me.' If you asked him what he neede reminding of, he wouldn't answer, leaving you to wonder what yo yourself needed reminding of.

You won't fail for being too outrageous. However, you may *fail for not bein outrageous enough.*

Stepping out of your comfort zone

If you're walking or intending to walk the hero's path down the Grea Thoroughfare, you'll be stepping out of your comfort zone frequently.

You'll find yourself in situations and with people that challenge a your concepts of reality. You'll find yourself doing things that shock an surprise you, not always pleasantly. You'll feel at times as though the te tonic plates of your reality are moving so fiercely that you don't knov how to place yourself. But without the psycho-emotional stretch tha comes with stepping out of the zone, it would be impossible for you t grow.

If you never went to the club that was playing the weird new musi where the people danced in weird new ways, you'd still be doing th twist.

And it's fine. Because when you step outside the zone, all you get i uncomfortable. And uncomfortable is only uncomfortable. That's a that's wrong with it. It isn't comfortable. The word literally means bein strong with (something). If you can only be strong if you're sitting in you

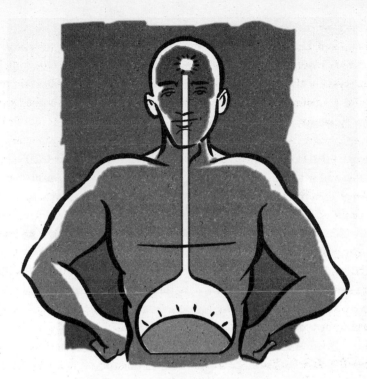

familiar chair, watching your familiar TV, drinking your familiar cup of tea and thinking your familiar thoughts, you've got a problem, as in an inner strength deficiency [see *Meditation* p.126].

If you can only be strong when the economy's strong, you'll be in trouble when it's in recession.

Imagine inside your body you have a flexible, unbreakable rod of two inches diameter, composed of a miraculously indestructible substance and emitting a constant, unwavering glow of extreme-brightness light, running from between your legs up to your solar plexus in front of your spine. When you inhale, you feel as if your breath is moving up the rod, and when exhaling, feel it go down. Each breathing cycle intensifies the light.

Do this regularly and you'll increase your core strength, and then no matter how weird things get, around you or within you, you'll feel strong with just yourself and neither outside factors nor inner turbulence will trouble you too much.

It might also be helpful, when managing discomfort, to vow to

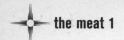

yourself, 'I will maintain. Until the walls come tumbling down, I will maintain. Until the stars fall from the sky, I will maintain.' (It's good to give yourself a bit of rousing from time to time.)

As it is likely that you'll be stepping out of your comfort zone with increasing frequency from now on, things being what they are on the planet, it helps to accept the following:

You, hero, must be prepared now to relinquish all comforts

Without being alarmist about it, the way things are going, hero or not, you'll probably have to relinquish all your comforts before you die, at which point they become irrelevant anyway.

It may sound horrific, but if it happens, it'll be fine. Because you'll handle it at the time.

Melodrama aside, the simple quest for fame and fortune may find you sleeping on people's floors or worse, before it delivers up the booty. You have to be prepared for that and sit relatively easy with the notion before you can be truly prepared for fame and fortune. Old timers call it paying your dues. No one gets away without it, at some time or other. It's what firms the psycho-emotional foundations of your inner structure, i.e. the self you have constructed.

Externally speaking, in the material world you can either have freedom or security. Internally speaking, when you free yourself of the notion of needing security you instantaneously discover an inner self-security that travels with you wherever you sleep tonight, cardboard box or Royal Suite.

Next time you expand outside the bounds of the comfortably familiar, allow the inevitable retraction that will follow, and notice, as you pull back into yourself, whether you've grown from the experience, spiritually, creatively and emotionally.

It's all there to make you love yourself more.

Don't resist.

Hero? You're a fool

You've got to be. Only a fool would undertake such a journey to find fame and fortune while the world shuddered in the throes of upheaval all around you.

The fool has been much maligned over the years. The term has pejorative overtones. But consider the qualities of the traditional fool, the archetypal fool as depicted in the Tarot deck, or in the Taoist image of the natural person/uncarved block. The fool is always at the start of his/her journey. The journey never gets stale. It begins again at every moment.

The fool is innocent. The fool is uncontrived. The fool is without guile. The fool has unquestioning faith in Divine providence and sustenance. The fool is without care. The fool simply follows the heart's fascination.

You always have to be prepared to make a fool of yourself. Especially when involved in offering your creative gifts to the world. But there's nothing wrong with that. Being a fool is beautiful if you surrender into it when it happens. Blushing is cute. It lets you and others know your vulnerability. It takes courage to be a fool.

It's good to practise fool skills, clowning, juggling, tumbling, talking gibberish, etc. because it loosens up the crust of respectability that forms on you when you get a bit stuck in your ways, and allows the hero room to breathe. Consider the terms hero and fool interchangeable from here on in.

Also consider conducting the experiment of dropping 'please' from your vocabulary for just one week. It's short for the antiquated 'if you please' and is actually redundant. If you ask someone to do something if it pleases them, you're asking the same thing twice. You have to trust that if it doesn't please someone to do something for you, they won't.

Be polite. Say 'thank you', but drop 'please' for one week and pay attention to what happens between you and the other person in the 'gaps' where you would have used it.

That's a fool's technique for triggering a mild, altered state during conversation time. Doing it may make you feel quite foolish/rude at times. But every so often, you do it, it works and a wonderful clear space opens up between you and the other person. And that's the point of being a fool. It's wonderfully clear when it works.

Taking daily action

Daydreaming's good. Visualising's good. Even essential. But actually stepping out of your imagination and doing something about it, out here on the planet, in real time, is what makes it happen.

Do not be misled into misinterpreting new-age wisdom, however treacle-sweet the manner of its delivery.

The inner work of visualisation, and the self-encouragement of affirmation sessions may well represent ninety-six per cent of the manifestation process. But nothing's actually going to happen unless you take action. Taking action is what activates the magic.

I could (and did) daydream/visualise what I'd like to say to you now, but only through my taking action this day are you able to read these words. And if I don't continue to take daily action in this respect, the book'll end up finishing here and we haven't even got anywhere near the juice yet. So I'm thinking I'd better hurry up. But you can't rush these things. I can edit later [see *Importance of editing* p.197].

Taking your day's action has to be done with today's energy. Yesterday's energy may have seen you lungeing fast-forward. Today you may be feeling more retiring, more passive. Don't push yourself. Always work with the energy you have. Do not try to repeat yesterday. Be how you are today.

Never push your energy.

Simply take action designed to further you on your path, the intensity of which is commensurate with your current energy level. This action may be a phone call/letter/e-mail/fax/homing pigeon/any other kind of communiqué. It may be a journey. It may be translating thoughts/pictures in your mind into lines, dots and squiggles on screen/paper, or into sounds in a studio/rehearsal/gig, or into physical movement in a dance/theatrical rehearsal/performance, or into film, etc.

There might be an action you could take at this very moment and come back to *Handbook For Heroes* at your leisure. Myself, I'm staying with it.

Taking risks daily

Impactful, effective action requires a risk. Your action might fail. Take at least one risk every day in connection with getting your message out [see *Confidence* p.31].

If, among the many things you have to do nothing springs to mind, think of the thing you're most afraid to do and do that, i.e. make the phone call you're afraid of/sit down in the chair and open the computer program you've been afraid of and write/design/compose/go and stick your flyposters up on the wall that's been holding you in dread, and climb the wall, stand on top and look around you (if you forgive the sudden flip from practical to metaphorical). Where do you go from here?

Making decisions – pendulums, Tarot, I Ching

When your familiar, tried, tested and trusted mode of decision making has gone on the blink and you've got a decision to make, and your mind's gone completely blank, swing a pendulum.

Pendulums

Any weighted object on a piece of string/cotton/chain will do. It's nice to use a crystal on a chain but a trainer held by the laces or a pair of headphones by the lead will do just as well. Hold the string/cotton/chain between the thumb and forefinger of your dominant hand so that the weighted object dangles freely over the upturned palm of your submissive other hand. Relax both shoulders, and with the weighted object held perfectly still, ask 'it' which movement signals a yes. Mostly this will be a clockwise circular movement. Then ask for a no. Mostly this will be a counter-clockwise circle. If you only seem to get back and forth movements, wait until they go elliptic then circular on their own.

Once you've ascertained the yes and no of the situation, you're free to ask your trainer/headphones/crystal, etc. any question of the yes/no variety you choose. For example: 'Would it be to my advantage to phone Riffifi Talula now?'

Then, on gaining an affirmative response: 'Will he be well disposed towards me and be inspired by my proposal?'

Then, on gaining another affirmative response: 'Was he actually christened with a name like that?'

Then, on gaining a negative response: 'Is his real name Riccardo?' and so on until you establish his real name is Richard Pickle.

So your pendulum-object can be used effectively to help you mirror your deepest intuition back to yourself.

You do nothing consciously to affect the movement. Unconsciously, the small muscles in your arm respond to prompts from your unconscious mind/higher self.

Your unconscious mind/higher self acts as a receiving dish, picking up all the information that exists in Creation from the vibrational waves surrounding and passing through you at all times, i.e. it knows everything, present, future and past.

Your conscious mind acts as a filter, selecting only as much information as you can actively process without driving your bicycle into a ditch, unless of course you intended to.

Swinging a pendulum is a way of overriding the filters to access the limitless knowledge of your 'own' unconscious mind/higher self, and thus assist you to make your decision. For a truly swinging experiment, try living by the dictates of your pendulum (shoe/headphones/whatever) for the rest of your life. Otherwise, use it whenever your mind goes blank and you've got to decide one way or the other here and now. The worst that can happen is you end up dead, but that's *bound* to happen anyway.

Tarot

Tarot cards are useful as a psychic CCTV. Frequent use is like having a monitor to watch what's going on behind the scenes of your life, where the otherwise occluded doings of other players in your story, lovers, business associates, etc. are revealed. *If* you know how to read the cards.

Something happens in the shuffling, cutting and peeling between your fingers, responding to your unconscious mind/higher self and the cards, which somehow sets them out in a particular order. There is an oscillation that must occur between visible reality and invisible reality which makes this happen. Which is a quasi-scientific/nonsensical way of saying I haven't more than a fleeting theory to explain the cards but they never lie, the buggers.

Avoid becoming obsessed with Tarot if you suspect your psychic structure rests on unstable foundations.

Practise detachment to enable relatively clear interpretation, and develop patience to wait and see what actually happens so you can say 'so that's what the cards were trying to tell me' as you fall off the cliff.

The Tarot provides an archetypal model for interpreting the signs around you and, though frequent use can derange you, throwing an open deck aimed at the occular region (eyes) of a rapist or other unwelcome attacker, can buy you valuable escape moments.

I Ching
The I Ching is a riddlesome old bastard of an oracle which, though rarely affording you a straightforward yes/no answer, will always take you a lateral step to the left so you can view your situation from another angle. This in turn may help you decide what to do, but probably won't. What it will do is remind you that whatever situation you currently find yourself in, it will change into some variant of its opposite before too long.

The I Ching contains buckets of sound advice for heroes. It is *the* hero's book (Taoist flavour), and is also useful for both propping up windows and hurling at unwanted intruders.

Of the three forms of above mentioned divination tools, the pendulum is the one preferred by the author because of it's quick, almost instant, it gives you a clear yes or no, and it fits in your pocket. Obviously on account of the Law of Chaos, the pendulum will probably mislead you from time to time, and don't blame me [see *Disclaimer and polite warning* p.5].

Is it possible for a hero to be part of a couple?
Anything's possible.

From time to time you get taken by the romance of the art form someone else has made of their life. Sometimes someone else gets taken by yours. Sometimes these two dovetail for a while, occasionally until the death of one or both of you. Sometimes this dovetailing results in progeneration of further potential heroes.

Things like this happen. The variables governing duration and quality of shared experience, however, are too numerous, and the range of possibilities that can occur so complex, that it would be intellectual conceit to explore this topic further in this context.

If broken down to the bones of the matter, the issue of personal/romantic partnership hinges, somewhere in the mix, on the sexual organs and activities of the couple.

Some heroes prefer to keep their genitals entirely to themselves. Others like to share them. The main thing is to be able to discriminate between fucking someone and fucking them over, attempting to stick with the former whenever possible while simultaneously aspiring to heroic ideals of integrity, honesty and kindness, and doing everything you do with love (no matter what).

Once you're dedicated to following your hero's path, nothing and no one will pull you off it for long.

If you can perform the miraculous feat of following your path in the company of an exclusive partner, and vice versa, for an extended period of time, without either of you compromising yourselves in a way that detracts from your integrity, fulfilment or excitement, you should really consider writing a book about it.

Is it right to capitalise on being a hero to attain fame and fortune?

Of course it is, if you want to be famous and rich.

Capitalising is not the same as prostituting yourself. Use everything you've got and can develop to further yourself along your path and in so doing, help others do so too.

If you don't want fame and fortune, or don't want them enough to justify the work, you can be a simple hero just making a living, living quietly and maintaining your sphere of influence and activity at low output/input level.

Otherwise, unless you've got something better to do, feel free to optimise, formalise, package and commercialise all the gifts you have to your hero's heart's content.

Remember, your spiritual life-lessons will come regardless, whether the scenery's glitzy or plain.

Making your life exciting for everyone else to enjoy

The world invents/elects role models, albeit just for a short while, to act as signposts that point to a desirable lifestyle.

By living your life in grand adventure style, you inspire others to do so too. The more exciting your life is for you, the more exciting it'll be for others to observe.

Naturally this puts you in line for the 'evil eye', the jealous gaze of others [see *Just say 'fuck 'em'* p.104 and *You can please some of the people some of the time* p.103], but if you cultivate your heroic qualities and pay special attention to modesty, the excitement you generate in your life in the process of getting your message across will inspire more than it incites to envy.

As a hero, one of your main functions is to inspire others, literally, to fill them with spirit, and you do this best by fulfilling yourself. After all, it's fulfilment, the filling of the empty space that everyone's after so, if you've got some and in getting your message across can teach others how by example, you'll be serving your society and culture.

In other words, your greatest act of service to society is to fulfil yourself creatively and to offer the fruits of your creativity with an open heart.

So you no longer need feel selfish for pursuing your dream. Far from it, you're a saint!

the
meat 2
Fame and Fortune

THE EXTERNAL AND INTERNAL APPROACHES TO ATTAINING F'N'F

The external approach consists of the visible actions you take and rewards you receive in the process of achieving your goals. Achieving your goal is the sole and primary motivation. Failure to do so equates to failure of your entire adventure, ensuing negative mind-states and self-esteem levels. Success in doing so usually results in an ensuing search for 'spiritual' meaning in your life. And there's nothing wrong with that if it makes you happy. But the need for it arises when the realisation dawns that the fulfilment of one goal leads directly to an empty space which can only be filled by the achievement of another, which process in itself eventually becomes meaningless and is ultimately unsatisfying.

The internal approach consists of reframing the entire picture into a spiritual context. Everything you do is part of a grand meditation. It's not the words you're writing as much as the psycho-physical satisfaction of tapping the keys and watching the words come up on the screen.

Your focus shifts from what you're doing to how you're doing it. You are, consciously connected to the rest of Creation, focusing on the pleasant feeling in your fingertips as you press down the keys and on the sympathetic connection you have with the computer and the words arise of themselves.

Your focus shifts from earning your bonus/promotion/reward/acclaim to how you're enjoying the job itself, paying equal attention to every aspect of the work, no matter how great or trivial.

It's not the result of the phone call, it's how much you enjoy the act of holding the receiver and talking/listening through it.

It's not the achievement of the goal, but the enjoyment of the process.

And if you ask 'what's the big deal about enjoying it?' I say the entire purpose of your being here is to enjoy yourself. And if you then rejoin that that smacks of mindless, selfish hedonism, I say that true joy only arises when there is harmony with yourself. And true harmony only arises when you're making full use of your gifts by cultivating and offering them with an open heart to a world with whom you stand in good relation.

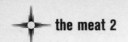

By following the inner approach, that moment of achieving your go[al], rather than being the big ra-ra with ensuing come-down, is just a flash[,] extra colour and brightness in the bigger picture. A bit of glitz to give y[ou] a titter.

The satisfaction comes from feeling relaxed and focused while y[ou] work, rest and play. This state is living in the Tao of what you do. Wh[en] you're in the Tao, what you produce will have true value, which will [be] obvious to others, and a demand for your product will arise of its [own] which, in time, if all aspects of promotion, marketing and administrati[on] are attended to in similar Taoist manner, lead you to achieve every g[oal] you set yourself as a by-product.

Intention and determining outcome

Just because you shift focus from goal to process oriented approa[ch] doesn't mean there's anything wrong with goals.

Goals are essential to making shape of your life.

There is a Taoist phenomenon called wu wei, meaning achieving go[als] without effort. The way you do it is by setting up an intention to achie[ve] say making seventy sandwiches in one hour, each one filled to perfecti[on] and blessed for the customer's benefit by your heroic self. Determini[ng] the outcome you wish to see, i.e. seventy mouthwatering sandwic[hes] walking out of your sandwich bar in paper bags, you then forget ab[out] the goal. You know that it takes about fifty seconds to make each one, [so] you relax into the psycho-physical process of spreading, filling, closi[ng] and slicing, and the enjoyment thereof, focusing on how excellently y[ou] perform each movement and pass. (The Tao of sandwich making.)

You set up your intention by seeing it done in your mind, and then f[or]getting all about that, you focus on executing the mechanics of [the] situation in as excellent fashion as you can.

Wu wei, however, applies to far more of a general spread of activit[ies] than simple sandwich making, and can be used to great effect and amu[se]ment with just about anything you choose to do.

The Tao giveth and the Tao taketh away

No matter how effectively you follow the internal/spiritual path of f'[...]

u cannot escape the cycle of ebb and flow (yin and yang) of said f'n'f.
The effects of fame and fortune come and go in waves. Don't cling to
em and that won't trouble you. Welcome the waves when they come in
d release them graciously when they leave. There's nothing you can do
stop the cycle so the only choice you have in the matter is in how gra-
usly you respond to its inevitable process.

Of course, it helps if you can divert a little of the second 'f' into some
nd of worthwhile investment situations to tide you over for low ebb
riods, just to even out your cash flow, but don't let that become the goal
itself because it'll dampen your creativity and push you towards the
n-heroic tip.

elcoming in the spirits of f'n'f

st like any other system of magic, Taoist practices include invoking
tities who reside without physical form in one or other of the invisible
mensions, commonly referred to as spirits.

Spirits may be simply thoughtforms (of your own or of others or both,
e Jesus, Mary, Krishna, Kuan Yin, Sid the Barber, etc.), they might be
tonomous beings in their own right, or they might be both (like pos-
ly Jesus, Mary, Krishna, Kuan Yin, Sid the Barber, etc.).

Whether they actually exist in a form you can prove is immaterial, if
u'll excuse the pun.

The moment you call up an entity, that entity exists, if only for that
oment, if only just for you. What is important is that in the moment
ring which that entity has validity for you, you as the invoker undergo
alteration in your conscious state. If, with full conviction, you call up
e 'spirit of beauty' for example, your mind state will alter a pitch or two
d you will see and experience the beauty of yourself and whatever/
omever you behold with more intensity. You may well be able to
hieve a similar effect by rolling dough if that's what you've chosen as
ur trigger mechanism.

If, however, you find yourself inclined from time to time towards the
agic-ceremonial tip, performing an invocation to welcome in the spirits
f'n'f will provide a quantum boost to the process of f'n'f attainment.

You can perform this discreetly and quietly to yourself anywhere, anytime, or you can make a whole business out of it and climb yo nearest hillock or mount dressed in your finest ceremonial garb ar shout it through a megaphone (or even mobile phone), staff pointing the heavens. It doesn't matter how you perform your magical operation as long as you do it with conviction, intent and self-unity.

Focus on the spirit of fame and say, 'Spirit of fame, I welcome y wholeheartedly into my life. Come in, make yourself at home and dor ask if you want to use the kettle, etc.'

You will probably experience a tingling in your consciousness as tl glitzzio-sparkly presence of fame enters your energy field.

Enjoy that for a moment and then focus on the spirit of fortune ar say, 'Spirit of fortune, I welcome you wholeheartedly into my life. N home is your home. Feel free to make any changes you like around t place, etc.'

Can you see the glittering diamonds, rubies, emeralds and gold, c you see the stacked wads of high-denomination notes of a relative stable currency, can you see the pile of deeds to your property portfoli Can you taste them? You will probably feel yourself being substantiate i.e. made more solid, as the etheric presence of wealth wafts into yo personal energy field.

Enjoy that for a moment, then say, 'Spirits of fame and fortune welcome you both to remain in my life and to grow in magnitude by t day/hour/minute/second.'

The results of this invocation are long-term but things should st; happening almost immediately. Signs will pop up (like Looneyt Entrance – you should've been more discreet!) to encourage you, peo[will start talking about you and money will come to you unexpectedl;

You can invoke the spirit of anything you like: health, longevity, sere ity, wisdom, love, sex, enlightenment, cashmere, humour, whatever.

Conduct refresher invocations when you feel the need, i.e. 'come ba you bastards!'

After a spirits-of-fame-and-fortune invocation session, gather yours back together again before proceeding with your life, and remember f' are only the fixtures and fittings of reality and not reality itself. Reali as far as your particular shape and personal formation are concerned, what you're left with inside yourself when you're sleeping out in the cold under the bridge in a boudoir of cardboard boxes and old newspaper. That's real. Anything more is a bonus, so never take it as a given.

Degrees of fame and fortune

Only the fame and fortune you personally enjoy at the moment of your birth are real. F'n'f are relative not absolute phenomena. Hence you can only have fame and fortune by degrees.

The degree of f'n'f-ness you aspire to is entirely up to you. The degree you actually need is equal to whatever it takes to prevent you starving/freezing to death tonight. Aspiring to the attainment of degrees above that is the game you play to keep yourself amused, i.e. from going stir-crazy while you prepare to die. Some heroes are comfortable aspiring and attaining to twenty-three degrees, others are uncomfortable with anything less than around ninety-six. (Figures supplied by Stats. Department of the Institute of Wayward Taoist Studies.)

Obviously the more degrees you require to prevent personal discomfort, the weaker your position is in the game.

The key to being a player is to vow to yourself that you will survive and thrive even if temporarily reduced to zero degrees of f'n'f. Playing from this standpoint affords you the whole spectrum of adventure experience and lends your life story the potential dynamics (light and shade) necessary to make it truly noteworthy.

Simply say to yourself, 'I vow to survive and thrive even if temporarily reduced to zero degrees of f'n'f.'

Whatever the degree of f'n'f you are currently enjoying, the way to proceed is to optimise on what you have right now.

Motivations for seeking fame and fortune

Power The more spiritually/personally evolved/developed you are, the more likely this is to be power over yourself, i.e. mastery/mastery, as opposed to power over others. If your motivation is for power over others, others (managers/agents/your 'public', etc.), by the immutable law of cause and effect, i.e. what you put out comes back multiplied, will end up having power over you to the degree you wanted it over them. If your motivation is for power over your self, then you're just using the whole f'n'f trip as a spiritual contex or gestalt for your evolution as a master/mistress (over yourself) and it won't matter to you intrinsically whether you ever actually gair the f'n'f or not. So you win either way. And everyone loves a winner especially the spirits of f'n'f who will feel far more disposed towards sleeping with you if there's no pressure to do so, just like any lover

Attention The degree to which you are spiritually/personall evolved/developed is the degree to which you desire to attend, i.e pay attention to your fellow creatures.

Masters/mistresses devote their lives to serving the Tao Creation, each in their own way. This often takes the form of serving fellow creatures in a way intended to reduce general pain/suffering levels and increase general relaxation/peace levels [see *The Five Excellences* p.121].

The less sorted you are on the spiritual/personal tip, the more nee you may feel for the attention of others. This usually takes the form of attention addiction. An attention addict has usually devised a se of complex manipulative ploys designed to draw attention, the mos extreme example of which is suicide, which usually achieves its end (pun) but is without benefit to the practitioner thereof.

If your motivation is the attention of others, you will be trapped b needing to focus all your attention on keeping their attention, i.e your focus will be on others but in a negative/fearful way.

If your motivation is to attend to others, to serve them by doin whatever you can as a hero to alleviate suffering and increase joy then it won't matter how much f'n'f you attain in the process because you'll be winning every time you smile and someon catches it.

Vanity You want the whole world to be your mirror and tell you hov pretty/handsome you look today, how desirable you are, hov accomplished and special you are. The extent you get lost in vanit is the extent to which you may later find yourself paying cosmeti surgery bills.

To escape the existential void The more spiritual connection you cul tivate [see *Meditation* p.126], the more you relish diving into the existential void. The more you do it, the more you see that the void is not empty, but is in fact the generating source of life itself, i.e. the Tao. The more you love floating and gliding in the void, dancing and cavorting in the undifferentiated absolute, the more magnetic/joyful/heroically magnificent you become. You become irresistible to the spirits of f'n'f, not to mention other people. Which, along with the rest of this Handbook is a very long-winded way of saying *meditation can make you very rich and famous.*

So you can say 'fuck you!' to the world. You can do this anyway, f'n'f or not [see *Just say 'fuck 'em'* p.104], but will quickly find yourself severely marginalised along with all the other spoilt children throwing tantrums in the playground (you naughty boy/girl) with chips on their shoulders, i.e. victims. This comes with seeking power over others.

To say 'bless you!' (Why, did I sneeze?) This comes with seeking to attend to your fellow creatures and has a much warmer flavour than 'fuck you' when it comes back around your way.

To escape from humdrum, mindless, brain/spirit-numbing workaday reality Quite understandable. And however spiritually/personally evolved or unevolved you have to be to want that, I'd say if you've got the urge, go with it (and sort the internal mess out later with a good therapist). It'll be worth it. You will, however, have to take a look at your inner self as soon as the f'n'f becomes humdrum. A master/mistress will see the majesty of Creation in all its complexity as much in the dull hallways of play-safe suburban houses as in the 'cutting edge' corridors of metropolitan culture.

To gain approval Until you approve of yourself, no one else's approval (parents/internalised parents/peers, etc.) will do it for you. And when you approve of yourself, you shine, opening the way for others instinctively to approve of you too. But you won't care because that's their business, not yours [see *Fame* p.13].

To get the girl/boy (according to gender status and sexual orientation of hero) And when you get them, you'll never know if it's you or your f'n'f they're after. Usually it'll be a combination of you and the f'n'f according to the personal depth levels of the girl/boy in question.

If you think you must have f'n'f to get the girl/boy, you must by extension also think you're lacking in some way without f'n'f. Stop thinking that or you'll never have f'n'f. By further extension, it must also mean you think you're lacking in some way without the girl/boy in your life. Stop thinking that or you'll never get the girl/boy.

A master/mistress cultivates self-completeness to the point where they feel self-complete without f'n'f or the girl/boy. Only in the state of self-completeness will your true self be clearly and undeniably visible to the girl/boy, then, if they like that, you've scored. If not, you won't care. What won't happen is that they try to fleece you. Firstly your aura/visible energy field will be too strong for any opportunist to feel safe around [see *Martial arts* p.138], and secondly, you'll be so clued in and energetically well informed that you'll see them coming.

The only way to get the real girl/boy, i.e. one worth knowing, is to be yourself. If that isn't good enough without f'n'f, it won't be good enough with it and lawyers will end up getting paid somewhere along the line. Stating the obvious perhaps. But if you can't state a bit of obvious about f'n'f in a book about f'n'f, where can you?

To generate fortune Having utilised fame intelligently and harmoniously to promote your product, i.e. you/your message, effectively, you generate enough fortune to be able to buy yourself a fully equipped sanctuary, away from all the noise and madness, for you and those you love, where you can undertake all the solo/joint creative projects you want without too much disturbance or financial pressure, i.e. serve your culture, and just come back into the madness for your gigs, appearances, meetings, interviews, or just plain old entertainment when you have to. *And* to go at *least* business class, if not first.

Now you're talking!

Time You spend your time immersed in spiritual awareness anyway and you can't think of any better/bigger/more entertaining game to play. (That's my kind'a hero!)

Take some time exploring *your* motivation for f'n'f. It will, unless you're either Superperson or Supershit, be a combination of factors such as the above. Your motivation will eventually trap you or set you free depending on how clear it is of personal vanity [see *Vanity* p.78].

From a spiritual point of view, the only worthwhile motivation is to spread love. The stronger you are in your love-spreading activities, the quicker the f'n'f will materialise for you. So get lovin'.

For a hero, it's simply:

The best game in town till the lights go out

Riding in stretch limos. Eating at the most fashionable restaurants. Dancing at the grooviest clubs. Attending the glitziest parties. Relaxing in the most exclusive vacation locations. First-class air tickets and lounges. Wearing the most sought-after clothing. Being photographed wherever you go. Being so popular you can hardly bear your own magnificence. Having a huge aura and being looked at when you walk in the street. People treating you like a god/goddess. Hanging out with all the other famous, fortunate people including leaders of countries. Causing a stir every time you make a public announcement. Reading all about it in the morning papers.

And you get to watch yourself [see *Meditation* p.126 and *Living theatre* p.40] throughout, as the planet rotates on her axis at a breezy thousand miles an hour, while orbiting the sun at a ferocious sixty-six thousand miles an hour.

You get to observe yourself throughout as the background drama of life on Earth erupts into ever new kaleidoscopic patterns of social, economic, ecological, political, geographical and ideological configurations.

And you get to watch yourself being afraid to lose it all, happy to have it all, getting attached to it all, getting detached from it all, being afraid you can't keep up with it all, marvelling at how well you're handling it all.

You get to watch yourself being strong, being weak, being up and being down, but all magnified and intensified in brilliant Technicolor, reflected back at you from TV screens and newspaper pages.

And all this as you glide in luxury around the surface of a planet that's carrying us to our probable dissolution as a species and guaranteed dissolution as individuals.

You get to see through the whole illusion of f'n'f, past all the glitz and glamour, past all the tawdry tackiness to the Tao in all its naked majesty, as it frolics behind the scenes of all this nonsense, from the best seat in the house.

Can you think of a better, more exciting way to amuse yourself spiritually till the lights go out?

Spreading light

The purpose of you being here is to enjoy yourself.

Your function here is to spread the light of your enjoyment far and wide (so others may see the light of your joy and remember to access their own).

It doesn't matter what degree of f'n'f you have [see *Degrees of fame and fortune* p.73], from check-out person to movie star, your function is to radiate your light in ever-increasing circles for the benefit of all others [see *Hardcore technique: Placing the star-symbol* p.136]. If you want to justify your f'n'f, this is the hook to hang it on. F'n'f allows you to radiate your light to more people.

Vanity

Vanity. Thinking it was you who made all this, your body, your personality, the world entirely on your own from scratch, thinking it was you who made things turn out as they did, believing in the myth of who you are. Vanity.

It's just a game of hide and seek you play with yourself. Vanity is the opposite of modesty. But do not be ashamed of it when you see it operating in you. There's nothing wrong with vanity. The Tao/your higher self will use your vanity to motivate you if that's the only hook it can find, so you can become a spreader of light.

So don't worry about vanity. Check yourself in the mirror. Go on enjoy it. Say to yourself 'I am beautiful!' That's it! (Just remember not to take it seriously or it'll trip you.)

Downside of fame

You can't be smelly in public any more. (Unless you want that to be part of the myth.)

The downside of fame, the loss of personal space/privacy, the distortion of your public persona and the sheer pressure of demand for your attention and time, is that it brings with it a new set of responsibilities.

Your first responsibility is to yourself. That is to be sure to respond to the fascination in your heart, follow it, and allow nothing to impede you. And to do at least the minimum necessary, i.e. exercise, meditation, good eating, sleeping, sex, company, study, work, etc., to keep your personal show on the road and self-supporting (financially).

Your second responsibility is to those around you, which extends to include all beings and phenomena with whom you share the world, especially children (especially your own), and anyone physically/mentally unable to fend for themselves currently in your care. That is to do the best you can in any given moment to preserve life, alleviate suffering and promote joy within the context of the situation in which you currently find yourself. You are not, however, responsible for anyone else's feelings. They are. This is not to give yourself permission to wilfully hurt anyone or thing.

The circle of life is eternal and unbroken, and all beings and phenomena owe their original creation and subsequent maintenance to the Tao.

Any pain you cause another with malice aforethought is eventually pain you cause yourself. If you pollute the atmosphere, eventually you can't breathe. As you grow, i.e. as your inner vision expands to encompass the infinity of Creation and you feel comfortable with that, you notice from time to time that your first and second responsibilities are one and the same.

Now you have a third responsibility to the myth you've created. Your image is now public property. People have appropriated your image along with the myth of yourself you've generated, more or less distorted by various journalists/documentary makers/professional and amateur general gossippers, and placed it somewhere in their personal cosmological map of the universe. They've lodged you in their own inner mythical model of reality. That's a responsibility. You've got to make sure you brush your teeth, shower, perfume yourself, be having a good hair day and look good in your kit every time you step outside because you're on duty. Should always do that stuff really anyway [see *Style* p.197].

Because you have the media platform to air your views, you have a responsibility to be precise with your message. Obviously everyone's allowed to talk crap once in a while, and do, but you must endeavour to keep this to a minimum so as not to waste valuable airtime/page space which could be taken up instead by someone who's got their precision flowing today and could use it better. You must be aware that anything you say will influence people and alter the prevailing cultural pattern to some extent and therefore have a responsibility to get your message across in such a way that light is spread rather than diminished.

You are responsible for the timetable you've constructed for yourself, for turning up on time or, indeed, turning up at all. If you make an arrangement, stick to it or at least be sure to rearrange it in good time. If you've agreed to appear in Berlin in November for one month, you can't go and catch the early snows in New Mexico without first clearing it with Berlin (and buying a ticket).

You are responsible to your Muse [see *Discovering and following your Muse* p.172], the source of the creativity which generates your fame, and must respond to its prompts in relation to whichever fields of creative endeavour you're currently engaged [see *The Five Excellences* p.121]. Sometimes it'll drive you mad and make you feel the need to split yourself in five to cope with the creative influx coming through the channel [see *Hardcore practice: Secret (no longer) Taoist energy control and visualisation mechanism for enhancing creativity* p.131]. Resist this urge. (Remember, you've got responsibilities!)

Take some time, say approximately two minutes thirty-eight seconds, to ask yourself if you're willing to take on all the responsibilities that come with fame.

Now tell me, even knowing there's a great possibility/probability that fame will fuck up aspects of your life you hold dear – privacy, love-relationships, friendships, self-peace, etc. – I bet you still want it. Of course you do, because it's the best game in town till the lights go out [see *The best game in town till the lights go out* p.77].

Developing role models vs. star-fucking

Appreciate and admire your heroes and always be ready to welcome new heroes into your life. (Heroes are your role models as you grow.) But do not worship them, i.e. give your power away to them [see *Being your own hero* p.35].

Socialise with your heroes when you get invited, but do not try to suck their energy by osmosis or to get your hero fix vicariously through them.

Hanging around places heroes frequent just to be around heroes, i.e. star-fucking, when you're not yet clear about being your own hero just so you can tell your friends the next day that you saw so and so, is a non-heroic pastime and will not further you in your quest for f'n'f.

Studying form, on the other hand, observing the hero's body language, style, delivery and social skills for purposes of self-modelling is useful for helping you to develop your presentation as long as you only use it for inspiration and don't simply copy, as that would be robbing yourself of your own hero-experience.

In other words, don't get caught up in someone else's message just because they manage to get their message out in a way you relate to. Don't use your admiration of them as an excuse not to bother with your own message-getting-out process. (Be your own hero.)

Fortune – the true nature of money as a medium of exchange

At the time of writing, a global financial/currency 'structure' of sorts is still extant. Money is a mythic substance. It doesn't really exist. Sure you can show me cheques, cash and cards, but they're just paper, scrap metal and plastic with no intrinsic value. You can show me figures on a computer screen and exchange rates in the evening papers, but they're just hieroglyphics of no intrinsic value.

It is universally agreed that these squiggles on the screen which can either enhance or ruin your lifestyle, indicate units of currency, the value of which, it is also agreed, is based originally at least on the value of gold, a metal with no other function than adornment and tooth-filling, itself having no intrinsic value save for that agreed on by us all.

Money is primitive magic serviced by a sophisticated supporting infrastructure: banks, stock exchanges, computer systems, cash cards, etc., but remains in essence nothing but a shared belief in a myth. The fact that we agree to uphold this myth and protect it with force when necessary, so far no matter how upside-down and inside-out things get around it, is probably as great a group-consensus contrick as you'll ever be likely to witness.

Money is merely (at the time of writing) the universally agreed medium of exchange for transactions of energy between people. If you make me a cabinet, Jesus or whatever your name is, and it takes you three days and a tree, and you decide that equates to eighteen units of energy, that means I owe you eighteen energy units. Now say you want a new donkey to ride into town on for Easter/Passover, worth, coincidentally, eighteen energy units, but all I have to offer you today is a bit of live healing and a pile of written words also worth around eighteen units, I take my healing and words down to the donkey-shop man on the corner who coincidentally needs some words to prop up a shelf in the bathroom and is willing to take the healing and put it in the freezer till he gets ill. I give him the healing and words. He gives the cabinet maker a new donkey. I take possession of the cabinet in which I place my antique thimble collection and everyone's happy. This example of everyday intellectual property/furniture/donkey-swapping, if multiplied by six billion, demonstrates the reason a medium of exchange like money is necessary.

Money is a magic trick, that's all. That doesn't mean you don't need any, though. However much of an illusion it may be, and however enlightened you consider yourself, if you haven't got any, you're fucked.

Anyway, I'm assuming you've got your basic money-earning faculties intact, based on the spurious idea that you had the money to buy this Handbook. If not, sort it out. What we're looking at here is not basic money-earning, though that at least will be a natural side-product of mastering the Five Excellences.

We're looking at making a fortune.

Say to yourself a few times, 'I'm looking at making a fortune', and see how good it makes you feel.

Money is a myth, an illusion. That is no less true for a small amount as it is for a very large one. Fortune is merely the nectar of the gods/

goddesses transformed into dots and squiggles on your bank statements. The mechanics of it arising in your life will vary from person to person, but all have their source in the Tao [see *The Tao giveth and the Tao taketh away* p.70].

If you take the information contained in the Five Excellences and manage to graft it on to your existing cosmology in a way that hangs naturally, if you perform the meditations and visualisations with enough conviction, if you've got the talent and *if* it's in your destiny, you'll make a fortune.

Fortune is relative. To one person ten thousand dollars is a fortune (especially if you've just had to pay it over for your kid's school fees), to another twenty-three million just gets you into the game. The point is to see the fortune you already have, even if it's only a little room and a bicycle's worth, feel appreciation for it, and set about expanding on that fortune.

Because money and hence fortune is an illusion/myth, it is highly responsive to the power of thought. If you can picture it coming to you, if you can picture it as yours, if you can smell, hear and taste the experience of being the person with that fortune, and if you can wrap all that imagery in a tight ball of pure energy with your mind, and hurl that ball into deepest, darkest space with all your might, until you can't see it any more, and wait until it bounces off some far-flung planet and comes back round your way again, and catch it, you will initiate an unstoppable process of fortune manifestation.

You already have a fortune – the entire universe is yours. All you have to do is reel the bastard in

Pick a number. Any number. The higher the better.

How much would you like your personal fortune to be worth? One million? Ten million? Twenty-three million? (Now you're talking.)

Decide on an amount, which you're perfectly at liberty to change (up or down) at a later date. That's the amount you have in your 'cosmic' deposit account.

It's yours.

See it written on a bank statement. Smile. Good.

Now all you have to do is call it in, as and when you need it. So if you need a new mountain sanctuary, and you reckon it'll cost you a quarter of a million to buy, and a hundred thousand to do up and equip, as well as needing thirty grand for a pick-up truck to keep there, you need a grand total of three hundred and eighty thousand for the project at this time. So you say to your own higher self (your own personal cosmic-banker), 'I'm withdrawing three hundred and eighty thousand as of close of business today.' You can even fill out a withdrawal slip if you're really into the ceremonial thing, but that's taking it a bit far, don't you think?

Now wait, and as you go about your regular routine, the three eighty five will materialise in time for you to do the sanctuary project. Or it won't. But what can you do? Stay in the city (and choke).

Fortuna, Lakshmi, Kuan Yin and you

The peasants of ancient Tuscany prayed to pre-Roman goddess, Fortuna, whence comes the word, for money, love and good fortune. I don't know how many remained in the peasant state or how many were financially elevated in status as a result of their supplications. I can, however, vouch from my own intercourse with her, that the odd prayer aimed in her direction does produce tangible financial-status-elevating results. You might try something like this: 'Fortuna, Fortuna, I'm not a crooner, but I'll sing you this little song. Send me a fortune, you old Italian goddess, and don't make me wait too long!'

Or:

You could try talking to Lakshmi, the Hindu goddess of fortune. Praying to her for anything you want often brings results, though obviously, as with all goddesses, not always, it depends on the time of month and other variables (witness many devotees in India who still haven't got a pot to piss in). Certain followers of Tantric yoga go as far as to visualise themselves making love with Lakshmi, believing that when she comes, she's so delighted she showers you with blessings and whatever you want. This also applies to girl-heroes, even though you might not admit to trying it, and that's fine – keep it to yourself. We don't all have to be blabber-mouths. So that secret's out (hope that's OK with Lakshmi) and if you try it, I can also vouch from personal experience that it works a treat.

If you feel so inclined, try that visualisation for yourself, being sure not to limit your range of imaginary free expression and when divine shudders can be detected, picture a fortune of everything you want heaped upon your humble person.

If the whole idea of that is too racy for you and you feel like reporting me to the blasphemy police, try this platonic version in Wayward prayer form: 'Lakshmi, oh, Lakshmi, you're the girl for me, send me a fortune, buckets of wealth, and send it as quick as can be, cheers, dear!'

Or:

You could conduct parlance with Kuan Yin, the Chinese Buddhist goddess/personification of compassion and good fortune. She's quite pure, a bit like the Virgin Mary, so don't you go getting no ideas now. Just say, 'All right, Kuan Yin, dump a fortune in my bin, dump a fortune in my bin, Kuan Yin!'

It doesn't matter what you say, goddesses and the like have a different slant on naughtiness than normal mortals and are not easily offended by the odd dodgy line or two.

Praying is only the envelope that carries the energy and intention of the person praying inwards (not necessarily upwards. Why do you always look up when you think of anything remotely divine?)

What you are praying to, ultimately, is your own higher self. Praying is merely the ritual to trigger your higher self/unconscious mind, itself one with the universal consciousness of the Tao, which responds instantaneously by not giving you a smack on the nose, and indeed may, in time, manifest your fortune for you as well. Don't take praying too seriously – it's merely a form, an activity, a method of connecting, but without the spirit that lies behind and activates prayer, your visualisations have no validity and will not work.

I sincerely trust this item hasn't offended any ancient Italian, Hindu or Chinese Buddhist readers and in no way wish for it to appear that this item is in any way intended to denigrate your goddess. And if I have offended you in any other way than a possible display of crassness of style, I say, lighten up dude.

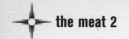

Receiving money for doing what you love

Do you believe it's possible to receive money just for doing what you most enjoy? Well, believe it, because as you believe it, so it will be, and believe that and so on. Not only is it feasible that you should receive money just for doing what you love, but highly likely. *Your best offerings come from doing what you love.* People can feel that love in your offering. All you have to do is package what you most enjoy so it's fit and ready for public consumption [see *Compositional skills* p.170 and *Presentation skills* p.180].

To begin or enhance this process, simply vow to yourself, 'I am now receiving a fortune for doing what I most enjoy doing. I vow to keep my heart (and deposit account) wide open to receive the fortune that comes to me' [see *Developing receptivity* p.94].

Excellence

Excellence, from the Latin meaning literally 'to rise above', is what occurs when you rise above, i.e. override, the self-limiting negative beliefs you hold about yourself (still?!) along the lines of 'I can't do it!', and simultaneously supplant them with self-affirming positive beliefs along the lines of 'I can do it!', following which you actually attend to that thing you have to do, say walking the Atlantic, no no, say doing the Tai Chi long-form [see *The magnificence of Tai Chi* p.144]. And rising above all turgid thoughts you let go into the form and fly.

That's excellence. It happens when you rise above your self-limiting belief.
(That's excellent!)

Commitment to excellence

If you want f'n'f, you must commit yourself, i.e. vow to yourself, to rise above all self-limiting beliefs you may be holding fast to, at all times and under all circumstances. Every action you take no matter how apparently significant or insignificant, you vow to take excellently.

This does not mean that you forbid yourself ever to make a mistake. No, you must be humble about it. When you're a prat, you're a prat, and there's nothing you can do but observe it and love yourself even more for it.

Over time, learn to let all your actions and deeds be an opportunity for excellence to occur.

Consistency

The only thing you can be consistent about is your inconsistency. That's what makes you so interesting (and drives all the girls/boys nuts – haven't you learned that yet?). Nevertheless you can achieve a degree of consistency between what you say you'll do and what you do. And if you vow to achieve excellence in all you undertake, you can also expect to do that (most of the time).

It is impossible to be consistent in your output. The tone and timbre of your creative outpourings are influenced by too many determinants (planets/hormones/moods/events, etc.) to expect consistency of tone, timbre and, shucks, even quality, let alone quantity. All you can expect of yourself is to be consistent in your commitment to following the path of your fascination, i.e. your Tao, like the true hero you are, wherever it may lead you, however far out of your comfort zone [see *Stepping out of your comfort zone* p.56] it takes you, in pursuit of excellence/mastery/mistressry in all you do and the f'n'f that comes with it.

You can also expect yourself to be consistent in your daily personal self-practice [see *Dedication of the hero* p.33 and *Martial arts* p.138] of those activities, both internal/meditative and external/active-exercise-doing, which give you the inner/outer strength, balance, health, clarity, creativity and faith to get and keep you going strong.

Over time, through disciplining yourself (sorry, no way round it!) to do what it takes to sort yourself out every morning before you start the day, you *develop unwavering resolve.*

By developing unwavering resolve, your determination to walk the hero's path to f'n'f, becomes unshakeable. Which is a pompous way of saying get on with it!

The nature of talent

Everyone's got a talent for something even if it's for appearing to have no talent.

All you have to do is build on that.

Talent, from the Latin, means having the sum of money necessary to enter the game. Later this came to mean ability to play the game (or piano, for example).

If you took fourteen four-year-old children and sat each down in front of a piano (you'd need a big room, a lot of pianos and earplugs), and if you then encouraged each to play in their own style and according to their own fascinations in sound creation, and if you were observant, sensitive and dare I say, intelligent enough a teacher, I wager you'd have the makings of fourteen fine pianists.

However, this does not happen, and there is neither time nor resources for talent to be fostered in each individual child equally. So some children, perhaps those with musical/musician parents or siblings or past lives as Chopin or Liszt, will excel at the piano, while most won't. But it's not that some are more talented than others. It's just that learning/cultivation facilities are not available equally to all children. No matter, they'll be good at football instead. At worst they can always be DJs [see *Musical instruments, recording studios (the Tao of sound)* p.194].

Cultivating your talents, i.e. your internal wherewithal to play the game as it appertains to anything you try your hand at, involves allowing excellence to occur [see *Excellence* p.86], and allowing yourself to rise above the self-limiting beliefs you hold to.

You can enter any game you choose. You have the internal wherewithal at your disposal. It's simply a matter of applying your focus [see *The stupendousness of Hsing I* p.150].

Simply say to yourself in self-affirmative, self-assuring tones, 'I have the talent to do whatever I choose with excellence.'

Nature of skill

Skill is the ability to organise information, whether physically/corporeally, as in moving your body in such and such a way to execute a dance or martial art move, for instance, or psychically/intellectually, as in shaping thoughts into a pattern first in your mind, and then on paper/disc/film/stage, etc. or in solid mediums such as stone/bricks and mortar/wood/metal, etc.

Skill relates to the crafting aspect of the creative process.

The art is to inform what you do so skilfully with your love of what you're doing, to breathe fire from your heart into your creation (like a god/goddess).

That's usually when people say you've got talent. Talent, skill, same thing really, just words (until you use them).

Training yourself

In developing mastery or skill, whether it's mastering jet lag on long-haul flights or mastering the perfect mix of your new tune, you *have* to undergo a (voluntary) self-training programme which enables you to practise through repetition the relevant moves and passes associated with whatever activity/field of activity you're currently focusing your attentions on.

When engaged in a self-training session, whether it's martial arts [see *Martial arts* p.138] or telephone technique [see *Telephone technique* p.189], and, as such, are temporarily operating as your own teacher (as well as own student), remember to teach compassionately and forgivingly, as you would a small child whom you love and respect.

Be patient with yourself.

Never feel you are wasting time by training yourself patiently yet persistently in new skills, however unrelated they may appear to be to the central theme of the plot of your life story at this time. Gaining mastery/mistressry (skill) in one area of action opens up your internal energetic pathways, as well as reinforcing your self-confidence to gain skill in other areas.

Overriding self-limiting blocks, i.e. self-pity

Concerning the attainment of f'n'f, or anything else you require for that matter, all thoughts that run something like 'I can't do it!' must be overridden and simultaneously replaced by thoughts that run something like 'I can do it!' Otherwise you're blocking the flow of good energy/information coming your way.

In carrying this into physical practice, say overcoming the block preventing you finding an agent to sell your manuscript, it is often effective to challenge yourself in a different, unrelated field of action, say jumping from a thirty-six-foot cliff past the jagged rocks into a small pool in the river below [See *Disclaimer and polite warning* p.5, esp. in the US].

Overcoming your fear of hitting the rocks will help you be fearless in phoning round for an agent [see *Dealing with fear of rejection/humiliation* p.100].

Or you could just cut out all the crap and phone round for an agent. (Come on, what's the matter with you?!)

The bottom-line self-limiting belief you hold to, which sustains all other self-limiting beliefs, is 'I'm here to have a shit time!' Say that to yourself and then stop that self-pitying nonsense and say, 'No, I'm not, I'm here to enjoy myself!'

Remember, that's your purpose here, to enjoy yourself. Think of a move you're scared to make, or an action which, if taken, could further you in your process of getting your message out, but which you're inhibiting yourself from making.

You want to enjoy yourself? Make the move!

Creating a masterplan vs. surrendering to destiny

One thing's for sure. We all have destinies. This can always be verified in retrospect but is obviously unprovable ahead of time, even though the use of psychic power to divine the future through oracles/visions/dreams is often effective for predicting certain outcomes [see *Making decisions – pendulums, Tarot, I Ching* p.61]. However, you're perfectly at liberty, and indeed are recommended by this author to devise a masterplan of your own.

If destiny is self-determined, the masterplan you devise will be your navigational chart to steer by as you sail through the future to the destinations of your choice. If destiny is a force you have absolutely no control over, then the masterplan is a pre-given blueprint, or map you're channelling to your predetermined destination.

The fact is, with all the wise twoddle we talk about it, no one knows the answer. It's probably a weird, fluctuating, complex weave of the two, all tied up with movements of moons and planets in our vicinity as well as solar-flare activity, not to mention the possibilities of chaos and random selection processes.

Nevertheless, it has been known to many a hero throughout recorded history that sitting in on a rainy/over-hot day to devise/channel/hone a masterplan can often prove to be a most useful and beneficent employment of time.

Plans should be laid out diagram style, as opposed to list style, so you can see what you're dealing with. Initially use paper. You can move on to canvass/screen, etc. later if you're that much of a masterplan fanatic. Use a large piece of paper so you don't have to cramp your vision.

Draw a visual representation of your long-term (four to twelve year) goal in the centre of the paper.

For example, you are the greatest living master/mistress of (wait for it) psychic taxidermy, all the world at your feet, every dead animal at your psychic-stuffing, fêted at the parties of the good and great, selling out Madison Square Gardens and causing traffic jams all the way up Seventh Avenue when you perform your extra night by public demand of live psychic taxidermy on stage, making it on to all the chat shows, quickly becoming a major sex-symbol in certain circles and adviser on matters of psychic taxidermy and suchlike to the president him/herself, who personally endorses the psychic salad dressing and associated products which you launch in a hail of acclaim and become the toast of the town in New York, London, Paris, Wolverhampton *and* Baden Baden. So you draw a shape to represent that, say, a stuffed stoat, in the middle of the paper.

Now draw a series of shapes in satellite formation around the central shape, each representing a different aspect of the work in progress or now being planned, which will lead to your attainment of the scenario represented by the central shape. One satellite, for example, could represent the university tour you have coming up where you'll be talking and demonstrating your technique to aspiring psychic taxidermists, or psychoderms, as they like to be known.

The next could represent, say, the recording session you've arranged to make a CD of psychic taxidermy tunes for meditation. Another could represent the marketing plans you have for that CD. Another could represent the psychic salad dressing project.

Once you have all aspects of the work representationally displayed before you on the paper, draw connecting links between them to represent the links that exist and which you would like to see exist between the various strands/shapes.

Now draw sub-satellites, i.e. moons connected to or in orbit around the satellites, each representing the various sub-plots you foresee being enacted in the process of attaining the central-shape scenario.

Now step back and take a look. If you don't like what you see, change it and feel free to do so as often and as radically as you like.

So there's your masterplan. Now you get to experience the amusement/bemusement of watching what actually comes to pass, and how much or how little resemblance it bears to the central-shape scenario.

If nothing else, it'll clear your head and may even turn out to be the first step in you becoming the most famous, if not the only, psychic taxidermist in the entire world. So watch out!

Opportunities

No one knows where opportunities come from, so we say they come from the Tao. It doesn't matter. What matters is, they come. And the more open you are to recognising that, the more frequent will be their coming, and the more valuable will be their content and import.

Opportunities exist potentially in every meeting you have with another person, because unless your career/social action hinges exclusively around animals, fish, birds, insects, reptiles, plants, trees, minerals or rocks (in which case, I'd *love* to know what actually happened in your head at the exact moment you chose to come in to town and buy this book), *opportunities come through other people.*

Hence, the more meetings of genuine substance you have with other people, the more opportunities are likely to come your way [see *Importance of networking* p.109].

Sometimes, when the planets are aligned just so, and your energy's flowing with force, you get bombarded with eight opportunities simultaneously, nine even, and may need to resort to swinging a pendulum to decide which if any to go with. Otherwise, try self-cloning.

If you like opportunities coming to you as if from nowhere, you might like to say the following in the bath/shower, while stroking your knees in clockwise circles (optional): 'I pluck opportunities out of thin air, such as opportunity-plucker am I. Opportunities come to me because I believe they do, that's why!'

Explore every opportunity that draws your fascination. As soon as you see a brick wall or cliff-edge to oblivion, drop that opportunity to make way for the better one that will inevitably rush to take its place.

Opportunities love you, because they need someone to come to through whom they can find their full expression. Otherwise, if not taken up, they remain in an undifferentiated, latent state, possibly for eternity, without ever seeing the light of day. So be kind to opportunities. See things from their angle. Give them a chance to express themselves, if only for their sake. (That's more like it.)

If you have experienced what you consider a dearth of opportunities in your life, it may be because you're not shiny enough. Perhaps your aura/energy field has grown opaque with the dust and grime of years of self-limiting doubt, and just needs a good polish. If they can't see your sparkle they often don't know you're there. They're funny like that, opportunities.

If you wish to polish your aura/energy field and make it truly sparkle so those opportunities come zooming in on you from miles around, avoid using common household polish as the consistency is too thick and mass too dense and it will penetrate your aura and fall directly on your physical person, causing hard-to-remove stains, etc. Instead, borrow from Native American tradition and use a smudge stick, which both cleanses and polishes in one. Smudge and go. A smudge stick consists of strands of sage, and often cedar and sweetgrass, bound tightly together, the end of which you set light to until, after much gentle blowing on the glowing end, volumes of illegal-smelling smoke can be made to billow about your person or about any object at which you choose to wave that smoking thing.

Watching carefully for flying sparks, start by smudging yourself, i.e. waving the smoke around your head, down your arms, over your torso, behind your back and down your legs, until your entire energy field has been doused in the smoke. If you are in company it is polite to offer to smudge them too. Then smudge your house or lodgings and belongings.

Sage purifies. Cedar banishes evil. Sweetgrass blesses you.

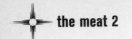

If no smudge stick is to hand, simply use your hand to effect similar passes in the air around your person, in order to signal to your higher self/unconscious mind that you want to give your aura a good spit 'n'polish.

A good, well-intended smudging generally boosts the frequency rate and value of opportunities coming your way. (*If* you believe it.)

Developing receptivity

All the opportunities in the world won't do jack shit if you're not receptive to them. Receptivity to goodness is an essential quality to self-develop, especially in the quest for f'n'f.

Sufis, mystically inclined Moslems, believe it is far more difficult to receive (love) than to give (it). So when they work on opening their heart centres, a practice around which much of Sufism revolves, they do it to receive love even more than to give it.

Kabbalists, practitioners of the ancient Jewish occult system for cataloguing and rearranging reality through various meditations and magical operations, and upon which system all Western (non-Jewish) occult systems are mostly based, pay inordinate amounts of meditational energy and attention to developing the will to receive. Kabbalah itself means 'that which is received' in Hebrew.

Taoists, and especially Wayward Taoists [see *Wayward Taoism* p.21] practise developing yin energy. Yin is the receptive element of the famous yin-yang partnership. In the advanced practice of Tai Chi [see *The magnificence of Tai Chi* p.144], practitioners work to develop 'receiving energy', whereby the opponent's on-coming force is received into an inner whirlwind of energy collected in the Tan Tien below the navel, to be instantaneously spun back out with eight times the original force.

Stand for a few moments with your arms held out, palms up as if to receive a huge gift from an invisible benefactor, i.e. the universe. Relax your chest and solar plexus (stomach) region and let go of muscular blocking that would otherwise impede the incoming flow of new goodness. Visualise new goodness, in whatever shape it may appear to you, rushing to fill your open embrace and say in self-affirmative tones, 'I am opening myself to receive new goodness. Come hither new goodness!'

You know everything. It's all a matter of where you direct your attentions.

I'm just stating the obvious. At least, obvious to me because I'm focusing on it now. But stating the obvious is my intention. And in so doing, my wish is for you to read this (enthusiastically tell everyone you know to read it too), and as you assimilate each item, say, 'I know that!'

Because you do.

When developing receptivity, it is also wise to develop gratitude and appreciation for what you receive.

Every time someone compliments you, rather than throw it away because your insecurities won't let you believe they mean it, say 'thank you' instead. Try it now. I'll be me and you be you. I say, 'Hello, you're wonderful!', and you reply, 'Thank you!' You have to accept the world's applause, in whatever form it comes, whether as a one-to-one compliment or acknowledgement or as a stadium's worth of cheering, foot-stomping, hand-clapping, woohwooh-whooping, yeehah-hollering fans.

Next time you're standing in front of an audience, try this for yourself. When the applause comes, stand (facing the audience) with your arms wide open, palms turned towards your audience, as if to receive. Relax your chest and solar plexus (and shoulders – oh, and anus if you can remember) and allow the energy of group love and agreement (for you and your message), i.e. applause, to penetrate fully to the very core of your being. Keep receiving applause, while simultaneously repeating the words 'thank you', which you allow to come from deep in your lower abdomen [see *Vocal training* p.186]. If the applause grows to a standing ovation, simply relax even more deeply and allow the love to penetrate deeper and deeper (until you come), say 'thank you' a final time, and walk off.

Well done! That was magnificent! You're wonderful!

And you say?

If the above scenario is difficult to arrange and you feel inspired to practise this exercise in receiving, arrange instead for no less than nine willing participants to applaud you vociferously for six minutes, their applause building to a stand-up crescendo of approval-madness, while you stand before them in the above-described stance.

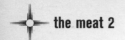

You've got to receive the applause, or what's the point of putting on the show in the first place?

Developing generosity

Generosity, from the Latin *generosus* (which is from *genus* meaning race) meaning to cause/produce/engender/generate, is the quality you draw on when you're in a state of generating energy solely for the benefit of others. The energy you thus generate may come in solid form as a gift/treasure/object of some form, or as information (energy in formation), such as a song you're singing to someone, or an idea/some encouragement you're giving someone. Generosity, being an active state of generating energy for others, is a fundamental aspect of the Tao, i.e. that which provides the generating power necessary to produce, inform and sustain (indefinitely) Creation, i.e. the universe and specifically at this moment, you.

By fostering your instinctual urges to generate energy for others, i.e. commit deeds of generosity, you align yourself progressively with the Tao.

Now, whether it's because the Tao is very nice, or just the workings of plain old cause and effect, or both, whenever you generate a portion of energy in whatever form for the sole purpose of gift-bestowal on another, that portion of energy will come back round your way, along with many other previously elsewhere portions of energy it's befriended on the way. It returns to you in time, usually from different quarters, exponentially multiplied.

You give someone a happy surprise, you'll get three back.

Save the life of one hedgehog in London and three marauding predators will spare yours next time you're sleeping in the jungle in Borneo.

Receptivity and generosity are just the yin and yang of the creative force of the Tao, i.e. Creation. You can't have one without the other (for long, without a major imbalance and subsequent disharmony occurring).

It is imperative to develop both qualities simultaneously to avoid imbalances in your life. A preponderance of generosity at the expense of your receptivity makes you a martyr, which is a most unimaginative, insipid path, and the fame it engenders will produce you no worthwhile fortune (you'll be dead). That's not spiritual, it's stupid. A preponderance of receptivity to the detriment of your generosity makes you a greedy pig. Being a pig, i.e. being in the extreme receptive position, does not prevent you being in receipt of fame and fortune for a while (there are many famous, fortunate pigs), but people will only want you for your money and power and they'll act like pigs around you (like attracts like) because, let's face it, you're a pig. Being a pig is not spiritual if you're actually a human, it's an aberration.

(Please note that although the author uses pig in the pejorative sense when applied to humans in nasty-greedy mode, he in no way means it to be derogatory to pigs, most of whom he likes very much indeed.)

It's about striking a flowing balance between the yin and the yang, between the receptive and the generous. So if there's a person you love lying in your arms, and you notice you're doing all the stroking, skin-kissing and caressing, lay back for a while and let them experience the joy of caressing you. Thus by being receptive, you're being generous at the same time.

In order to develop generosity, over the next twenty-eight hours find something you like in three different people and tell them; pay genuine compliments to three people, without concern for their response.

Think of up to eight hundred people at a go and wish them all well.

Think of up to nineteen thousand people and wish them all well.

Think of all the people on the planet, and not only them, but all the animals, including rats, all the insects, fish, birds, etc., and all the plants and trees, and wish them well.

Remember to continue to develop your ability to receive on a daily basis [see *Developing receptivity* p.94] so you can catch those wishes of wellness when they come round back to you.

How big you go with your generating depends on how big an arena you need to act out your life story to the full. The more generous (*and* receptive) you are, the bigger the arena you'll have to play in. In other words, the more you interact with others in a life-affirming/supporting way, the more people like dealing with you, and as your popularity spreads, your sphere of influence and activity expands with it, which is the basic mechanism of the f'n'f attainment process.

According to the biblical rules of tithing, if you give ten per cent of your time/energy/money away every day/week/year to people/groups of people/even animals/birds/fish/insects/trees/forests, etc. who need it, you'll keep the energy flowing freely in your life to the benefit of your bank balance.

The Kabbalists say never give away more than twenty per cent of what you have or it'll weaken the flow.

Wayward Taoists simply say balance the yin and yang (but not without writing a whole book around it).

Touching forefingers to thumbs thus forming little circles of space between, buddhas when giving audience would sit with left hand pointing down and right hand pointing up, both palms turned towards their assembled company, in order to receive energy (freely) with the left and give it (generously) with the right.

Try this for yourself the next time you're giving audience, and wish to focus on developing a balanced through-put of yin and yang, but best keep it subtle/discreet, or they'll just think you're a prat pretending to be the Buddha [see *Let them call you pisher* p.101].

A nice game to play with the Tao (who loves a nice game, it should be mentioned), is to rush about being generous in thought, wish and deed for one week to everyone and everything you encounter, and thus build up a stack of credit. Then stand back for a moment, give the Tao the nod and wait for it all to come bouncing back to you (multiplied).

The immutable universal process of cause and effect, karma, yin and yang, do-unto-others-etc., what-goes-around-comes-around, or however you want to call it, is an ever-returning circle. There is never a time that this is not true.

It is essential for your future well-being, therefore, to balance this with the central ethos of Wayward Taoism. 'Do whatever you like and not only get away with it, but be loved even more for the doing of it.' [see *Wayward Taoism* p.21].

Following your creative impulses

Developing receptivity and generosity also applies to your relationship with the divine realms whence comes your creativity, i.e. the Tao/Muse.

Being receptive to creative impulse in turn requires that you be generous enough to that impulse to give it life by crafting it into a usable shape, by writing/drawing/recording/filming/sculpting/painting, etc. it in noteform immediately.

Do this with every creative impulse you are receptive enough to be impelled by, and maintain explorations until you lose interest.

Thing is, if you don't have a go you'll never know.

Having the courage to give your creative gift to the world

It does take heroic courage to stand before the world with your creative offering held aloft and proclaim boldly, 'I have this!' You must always acknowledge yourself on that account every time you do it, successful or not.

But look, the worst that can happen is that everyone you show/read/play/perform it to, tells you it's crap and you're crap for doing it, and then proceeds to institute a global ostracisation programme to the effect that you are now banished from the realm until you grow old and feeble enough no longer to pose a threat to the good taste and sensibilities of decent folk and when, after a lifetime's exile, you finally return, anyone who's still around that remembers you crosses to the other side of the street, and you end up lonely and miserable, dying.

But the chances of things getting that bad for you are really quite slim [see *Being courageous* p.54].

On the other hand, it's not beyond the realms of good reason that those to whom you initially present your creative offering may be more generously inclined towards you. Perhaps they'll just *think* it's crap, tell you it's great and then tell everyone else it's crap. Though this is a common occurrence it is also possible that they might actually like what you've done.

Once you've got your creative gift/message-to-the-world clear and well-formulated, packaged and presented to a degree you, at your present stage of evolution, feel comfortable and delighted with, take it proudly (but modestly) into the market place/world/general affray and offer it courageously with an open heart.

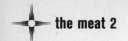

Dealing with fear of rejection/humiliation

Welcome every rejection as a sign that you are one step closer to your goal of having your gift received by the right pair of hands, metaphorically speaking. It just may be that this particular project you're working on has a certain quota of obstacles pre-allocated to it. So the faster you work your way through them, the quicker you get your project through.

It is also important to remember that universal liking for your person/product is highly unlikely and probably impossible. One person's hero is another's anti-hero. One person's masterpiece is another's pile of crap. Moreover, a person, you yourself, may have loved Mozart with an overwhelming passion this morning, yet even his music makes nothing more than an infuriating noise this evening.

Take opinions with a pinch of salt (including your own). Don't take rejection personally. Take it transpersonally, i.e. rather than thinking what a stupid donkey you are, be enlightened/spiritual about it and think instead what a stupid donkey they are.

Welcome humiliation as an opportunity for you to experience the shame of being seen to be wrong/stupid, subsequently to discover that it didn't kill you, you're still here, in with a chance, and grown one big portion less afraid of humiliation. The dunce in the corner is just another role you get to play from time to time in the living theatre and is, if surrendered to, a time of extreme grace. In other words, humiliation makes you stronger. You could let it kill you, but what would be the point?

Not getting suckered by other people's reality/myths

You create your own (experience of) reality. Other people create their own (experience of) reality. Do not get the two confused.

This week, someone who managed to get their unique message through with integrity did it using a washboard sample and a few lyrics sung in broken Welsh, so now all the A'n'R people want washboard samples and broken Welsh because *that*'s what's selling. Some might even encourage you to be original, and suggest you use an ironing-board sample instead, but that's just their experience, i.e. view of the way things are.

The person who made the washboard sample song wasn't thinking this is going to be commercial, he/she was just using the washboard to express their truth, because that sound represents *their* experience/view of the way things are. Let your creative gift come from your soul responding to the experience of reality *you've* created, and not be a gift that comes from the part of you that needs the approval of people who think washboard samples are commercial this week.

Thirteen people may tell you that the industry's dead at the moment and you'll never get your project accepted. But if *you* see a picture of the powers-that-be signing that deal with you, then go forth and offer.

You may be wrong, of course [see above *Dealing with fear of rejection/humiliation* p.100], and if you are and later catch those same thirteen people sneering and sniggering behind your back, you may draw sustenance and find relief from your upset and shame by following the following:

Let them call you pisher

An extremely wise, much-loved, learned, kindly and respected, old, dead, latent-Taoist, Jewish man, who also happened to be my grandfather, when threatened with humiliation as in when being warned 'they'll think you're stupid', would always say, 'So let them call me pisher!'

Pisher is a Yiddish word which can only be inadequately translated as someone who wets their own pants, with all that implies. In other words, one in the role of dunce in the corner.

What old Solly was saying (according to my own projections) was, it doesn't matter what other people think of you, because *before, above and beyond anything else, you've got to respect yourself.*

If you wish to try this approach to dealing with fears of humiliation which might be blocking you from coming through, but feel uneasy with the ethnic idiom, you can substitute pisher for any other derogatory nomenclature you like. Try dickhead, bumhole or asswipe, for example. But they just don't have the same finesse [see *Style* p.197].

It must be noted that this item drawing for its substance, as it does, on immigrant Yiddish wisdom, does not constitute any part of traditional Taoist philosophy, even though Lao Tsu and Solly are probably the best

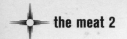

of mates these days, but falls solely within the philosophical 'confines' of the modern Wayward School of Taoism.

Feedback

Every yes and every no you encounter on your journey to f'n'f, feeds back information to you, some obvious, some discreet and registered in your unconscious mind only.

This information triggers emotional responses, such as joy or anger, depending on the yes- or no-ness of that piece of feedback. These emotional twists and turns in relation to the creative project you're currently working on add the necessary spice/grit to the mix, without which your work would be just so much schmaltz (American showbiz Yiddish vernacular for sickly, overdone, middle-of-the-road, over-sentimental pap of no artistic merit whatsoever).

Feedback is essential to honing your message.

Feedback from judiciously wielded electric guitars has always enjoyed a hallowed place among the favourite sounds of 'modern' mid-to-late twentieth century popular music. Allow feedback from the world to wash over and around you in the same pleasurable way as would a nicely mixed-in sample of guitar feedback (as opposed to some nonce with a guitar actually doing a live Jimmy on stage), gently honing and weathering your message into shape so it has a context in which to travel.

Saying no gracefully

As your message grows louder and clearer and starts to attract many new people into your orbit, you will be offered many opportunities and will receive many invitations to do this or that. Many of these will require you to decline. When doing so, it is always prudent to do so graciously.

This involves speaking from the heart, or making a plausible facsimile of same, and saying, 'Thank you, I'd love to, but I must say no.' If your declining is not readily received, repeat the above phrase, inserting simply, as in, 'I'd love to, but I simply must say no.' This is best accompanied by a smile, neither too broad nor too mean, but firm, unwavering and compassionate, and be sure to hold the gaze of your rejectee and not look sheepishly down or away while giggling stupidly.

In time, you'll be able to imply that whole sentence employing only a simple 'no', and with enough practice, you'll be able to dismiss all undesirable invitations merely by clucking your tongue once against the roof of your mouth, turning your head slightly to the side and looking at the floor, as is often customary in the Middle East among girl-heroes.

Practice saying no gracefully into a mirror, until you feel positively charmed to be rejected by yourself in so kindly and self-assured a manner. Then practice it next time someone issues you a potentially bogus invitation.

Sometimes, however, even the most experienced hero finds it inexpedient or embarrassing to say no, and resorts to being flaky. Do not be harsh on yourself if this should occur from time to time. Simply breathe and observe without judgement, and in time gracious nay-saying will come naturally.

You can please some of the people some of the time

But it's better to focus on pleasing yourself and the rest usually follows. Naturally it is pointless to attempt to please everyone, as everyone has different tastes, moods and requirements from moment to moment and the variables are too complex even to begin considering how to please that person consistently, let alone six billion.

Do not take it personally when someone *is* not pleased by what you currently have to offer.

Do not take it personally when someone *is*. What pleases them at this moment is entirely and exclusively an aspect of their personal, particular evolutionary/developmental process, and has nothing to do with you.

What you have to offer may sometimes coincide with what someone wants, or it may not. It's more to do with averages than personalities.

So the best you can do is please yourself within the bounds of legality, free will of others concerned and basic human decency, and let others please themselves. If it should so happen that what you offer pleases them, so much the better. If not you could always try following the following piece of advice:

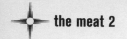

Just say 'fuck 'em!'

Sometimes the most expedient way to deal with rejection, humiliation or disagreement, i.e. the way that will best enable you to stay effectively focused on the job at hand at that particular time, all things considered, *is* to say, 'fuck 'em!'

This technique is useful for dealing with both the outside world and your own self-critical thoughts [see *Shoot the critic* p.28]. Every time you imagine someone criticising your project/work/output/self, feel free to repeat the mantra, 'fuck 'em!'

This, however, is not a foolproof way of dealing effectively with all disagreements; indeed, saying 'fuck you' aloud to other people should be avoided, and its use limited to special occasions [see *Martial arts* p.138].

Paradoxically, fucking, sexual intercourse, is right at the top of the charts of people's favourite things to do, and, though superficially disguised as an insult of the highest order, 'fuck you' is obviously, in reality, a blessing. Sexual intercourse is (potentially) one of the most exciting, pleasurable and satisfying experiences on offer. It's what people fight for, kill for, pay large sums of money for, work out in gyms for, become heroes/heroines for, risk their lives for, and even get *married* for. It also produces brand new people as if from nowhere (the Tao). That's how special it is. And it's that specialness you're unconsciously wishing for others every time you say 'fuck 'em!' It's important to know this because what you wish for others comes back on you multiplied.

Always be clear about the energy you're sending out.

In time, you might find it preferable to cultivate the habit of saying 'bless you' in its place. At first try it when people sneeze, and then start branching out until you're able to say it to anyone at any time without appearing like a pretentious new-age pillock.

Saying thank you gracefully

As your message spreads further afield, the incidence of people paying you compliments increases.

People love to acknowledge you when you shine, whether for your work, achievements, your appearance, or your qualities. It is your responsibility as a hero to allow them to do so. To deprive them of that

104

pleasure by being dismissive, churlish, falsely modest or coy, on account of your own insecurities and low self-esteem, is not only mean, but is indicative that you're blocking the flow of good energy coming your way [see *Developing receptivity* p.94]. The only heroic way of receiving a compliment, even if it is insincere, sycophantic, or greasy flattery, is to say, 'thank you!' This must be accompanied by full eye-contact. Sincere smiles are optional.

If your complimentor persists to the point you think it's getting silly, extend 'thank you' to 'thank you very much'.

If that doesn't do it, extend that to 'thank you, thank you, thank you very much, you're very kind!', which always seems to do the trick because they finally feel acknowledged back.

This applies also to the Tao/your own higher self, who compliments you daily by not dropping an asteroid on your head. Try saying 'thank you, thank you, thank you very much, thank you, you're very kind!' as often as you can remember. Of course this will mean absolutely nothing to the Tao who, if it thought about it at all, would probably think you're pretty silly talking like that, because it's doing its Creation-generating project regardless of whether you're grateful or not, and is certainly not doing it all just to please you. But it's good for you to say thank you because it makes you more receptive.

Also remember to say thank you to everyone who helps you in any way at all along your path to f'n'f, even and especially if you know them really well.

Myth of 'the public'

There really is no such thing as the public, except as an idea in your mind. Gathered together, all the members of the public (as you see it), form a (very) large crowd and, when viewed from afar, do indeed appear as if they form a solid mass. As you approach them, however, on closer inspection, the public, from the Latin meaning people, can be seen to be just that. Six billion individual people. Each with their own personal and unique universe of thoughts, beliefs, ideas, memories, expectations, desires, dreams, attachments, loves and agendas.

Cultural trends occur when enough people agree on the validity of a certain product/group of products/style of product. They arise when the sales of that product reach critical mass, i.e. burst forth into the mainstream, and often take on the appearance of an international institution, like say certain fizzy poison-drinks/toxic-hamburger chains you know and love, at which point it could be said the 'public' approve of that product. But that public is composed only of many individuals who just happen to agree for a long enough period of time on a particular trend. And you're one of them. Do you feel like part of the public? No? Why, just because you're sitting in your own space and not out playing in the crowd? No. It's because you're an individual.

For the sake of psychological convenience and marketing expedience, however, we agree to uphold the illusion of 'public', just like we do the illusion of money. We agree to delude ourselves that we're part of the public when we're part of the crowd, i.e. when we're playing the role of punter/customer/consumer, and we agree to delude ourselves we're playing/performing/writing/talking to the 'public' when in the role of the one offering the entertainment for the night.

But in reality, it's all make-believe.

There is no public, just lots of individuals. So there's no public to please, just lots of individuals. And as it's impossible to please even yourself for long, let alone someone else, how can you even consider pleasing lots of them? Forget it. And focus instead on doing what you most enjoy. From that will spring the information you need to formulate your message, which will, in time, if conceived, presented, packaged, promoted and marketed effectively, bring pleasure to vast numbers of individual people. As for the public and your fears and misconceptions thereof, simply think of all the individuals in the world and say to them (in your mind, or over a microphone plugged into every TV/radio station on the planet if you can arrange it), 'I love you all! I really do! I'm standing here before you now, so you can love me too!' (If you like that kind of thing.)

Gaining agreement for your idea

Everything here starts with an idea, even you, as in your dad getting the idea to make love to your mum that night or day you were conceived.

Everything from a computer chip in the corner of a matchbox to a sky-scraper in a large metropolitan area starts (and is sustained) with an idea.

The idea *you* have will probably change the world. But first you've got to get people's agreement to endorse your idea for it to gather force and travel.

That's all you have to do. Get one million, two hundred and thirty-three thousand people to agree with your idea and you've got f'n'f (providing you do a good enough job of packaging, promoting and marketing the idea).

Agreement spreads in a series of quantum leaps, like standing at the centre of an ever-increasing number of concentric circles, each one exponentially larger than the one before. It starts, however, with you agreeing with yourself, moves from there to one other person, to two, to four and so on.

You bought this Handbook, or the person who bought you this Handbook bought this Handbook because you/they agree with me that it's worth a read. You may not agree with everything contained herein, i.e. the content, but you agree with the context, i.e. the idea of presenting weird old Taoist shit as if it was something fashionable and groovy.

You tell your friends about it (enthusiastically), until they all agree with you/me too. Then each of them tells all their friends (or enemies depending on what they think of the book), and so its reputation spreads in exponentially expanding circles.

Importance of developing steadfastness

You dream up a project. You gain your own agreement about it. You tell a friend. They encourage you. You tell another friend or two. They like the idea. And with the sound of general consent in your ears, you make a contract with yourself to carry the project to a successful conclusion. You set to work. A few days in and you become aware of the immense workload involved. Momentarily, you feel afraid of having taken on too much. You feel inadequate. You start to doubt the validity of the project. You know it's a good idea. But maybe you're not up to it.

You're wobbling.

Stop that.

You've got to hold steady on your projects even, and especially when, you get the wobbles.

Giving up when you know it's pointless going on is expedient.

Giving up while in wobble-mode will merely set up an extended wobble cycle in everything you do. Ride wobbles like waves. You don't jump out of a speedboat because it wobbles on a wave, you sit down and steady yourself.

Handling public adulation addiction

Occasionally you hit on an idea that takes the imagination of people in such way they start to adulate you.

This usually intensifies around the time you're promoting a new product, a book, a CD, a live tour, whatever, and you're doing the PR rounds, chat shows, radio interviews, journalists and all that ra-ra.

You get invited to parties and people there adulate you. You walk down the street in the centre of town and people there adulate you. Three, four nights/days of that in a row, and you start getting hooked, albeit their adulation is a hollow phenomenon [see *Fame* p.13].

This is the early stage of public adulation addiction syndrome (PAAS), which often arises after an attack of public acclaim overload (PAO) [see *Disadvantages of being a hero* p.23]. You don't want to go home and be alone. You don't want to be quiet. You don't want to look inside yourself. You just want more adulation.

To antidote PAAS, you first need to be aware when it's happening. Without inhibiting yourself in any way, continue to mingle with your fans, while simultaneously paying attention to observing yourself. Watch yourself drinking in the adulation, sucking it up like a hungry baby on the tit. Because that's the level PAAS operates on. It's the unsatisfied baby inside you who needs more and more. (Obviously this applies equally to all compulsive addictive disorders.)

The next thing to do is the equivalent of taking an unexpected cold shower to wake yourself up. At the zenith of the night/day's adulation/receiving session, just when you're getting so many compliments you can hardly stand up [see *Saying thank you gracefully* p.104], suddenly disappear. Slip out unnoticed and go home. Be alone. Be quiet. Leave the

CD/e-mail/answerphone/telephone/mobile phone alone and do nothing. Simply sit being no one special. Just someone alone in their home doing nothing. And breathe. Breathe deeply and regularly until after some moments you remember that the source of all your fulfilment is inside you [see *Meditation* p.126].

By emptying your mind of the swirl of the social whirl you once again enter the inner void, whence springs the energy that sustains you, compared to which even the undying adulation of eight point nine million people is merely a tawdry conceit [see *Vanity* p.78].

Repeat this often – suddenly, unexpectedly, anonymously leaving parties/clubs/gatherings, etc. at the point of the highest enjoyment. Stop at the top.

After a while you will feel equally nurtured alone or among crowds of adulators.

If the condition persists and you find yourself over-extending partytime just to satisfy your adulation addiction, to the detriment of your creative output, go and visit your nearest healer/barefoot doctor for a sharp thwack on your occiput (back of head) with a medium-size stick.

Importance of networking

You do not work in isolation. Even if you're an author sitting on your own writing a book. To check whether you're on beam, you need people to read your material to, who in turn give you the various levels of feedback/encouragement you need to go on (or stop!). To sell the book, you need agents, publishers, PR people, bookshops, and finally people going into bookshops and buying the book. Then you need all the subsidiary/auxiliary business, banks, graphic designers, accountants, lawyers, dentists, healers, and whoever else to keep your show on the road.

It's nothing to be ashamed of. Admit it. We need each other.

You need others to spread the word for you and introduce you to other people they know who can help you. There is nothing wrong in using people in this way. That's what you're meant to do. Conversely there's nothing wrong with allowing yourself to be used likewise. It's good to be of use. It's *ab*using people and allowing yourself to be abused that's no good, no good at all. But using is good. Or you can call it networking.

Networking is fun, and gives you something to do at otherwise boring parties/clubs/gatherings. Network for others as much as yourself [see *Developing generosity* p.96].

Take pleasure in introducing people who may be able to help each other. If Bipsi Wà wants Isq Idad Rudriga to play on his recording, and Rudriga's manager is sitting over there, put the two of them together so something might come from it even if there's nothing in it for you. Be generous with your connections and all the opportunities they potentially offer each other. Put energy into spreading opportunities for others and it will come back on you multiplied.

When you shine, you shine, and when you don't, you don't

To network and socialise effectively, you need access to a good working personality, preferably your own, an absence of hostility/bad-breath/untoward body odours, clean fingernails and hair, and suitable apparel [see *Style* p.198].

And you need sparkle, otherwise known as shine.

Sparkle or shine is a mysterious substance. Commonly known as charisma, it's the light that surrounds you when you walk in the room. It originates deep inside you, and has nothing to do with your hair (or anything external) that day, though obviously it's harder to shine on a bad hair day because you may not feel so confident [see *Confidence* p. 31].

Charisma, sparkle, shine grows in proportion to how relaxed you feel, which is why daily meditation and/or martial arts practice, regular visits to a healer and/or self-healing sessions are vital, as is having adequate sleep on a nightly/daily basis. You can augment these aids to charisma reinforcement by saying the following affirmation: 'I shine in a line from my head down to my toes. I sparkle like a diamond, wherever my good self goes.'

Sometimes, though, no matter how well meditated/martial arted/healed/slept you are, you still feel flat. You've probably got a cold, flu, one of those nasty viruses or a period coming on. When you're tired/stressed and your immune system is working harder than usual to maintain internal homeostasis, the blood in your liver tends to become deficient, and that causes dullness in the eyes, hair and skin, as well as making you feel shy, awkward, introverted and depressed.

Eating a raw beetroot at lunchtime as a liver-blood tonic will often bring some sparkle back in time for the evening.

If, however, you find yourself in a potential networking situation, and you're feeling shy and awkward, say to yourself, 'It's all right for me to be feeling shy and awkward!' And then just be shy and awkward. Don't let that stop you, though. Simply be a shy, awkward person doing networking. You're allowed. It's really OK to be shy. What's important is that you relax with it and into it. Relaxing, breathing, self-observing, feeling vulnerable, feeling shy but valiantly networking on. That's good.

If that doesn't work for you, go home and get some sleep.

(You get days like that.)

Cocaine as a social/personality stimulant

Though it's perfectly natural, normal and even important for your self-development as a hero/human to feel shy and awkward from time to time, many heroes/anti-heroes on the quest for f'n'f, during phases of intense networking activity feel the need to mask their insecurities from self and others by using anaesthetic, i.e. cocaine. This can be attested to by the endless stream of people in pairs making bee-lines towards the toilet facilities at parties, clubs or restaurants with determined, fixed facial expressions, and returning shortly thereafter with large grins and talking loads of excitable nonsense, the sub-theme of which is how great they are, sniffing and sometimes picking obsessively at their teeth.

It has often been said that cocaine is a loser's drug. I would qualify that. When you're doing charlie (devil medicine), your aura/energy field grows darker, your heart centre closes down, your love stops coming through, you start to hate yourself, you become paranoid, you lose self-respect because you start believing you can't socialise or face people without it. You harm your liver and you lose your sparkle – so you find it harder to socialise, so you take more, you become abrasive and put yourself in league with devils.

Not that that will stop you. Just be aware of the power of what you're playing with and pay extra attention to practising meditation, martial arts, exercise and healing by way of compensation. Also take the herb

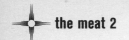

milk thistle to ease your liver and gently snort a mixture of one part lavender oil, nine parts lukewarm spring water up your nose in the morning to help soothe your nostrils.

By darkening your aura and energy field, you open yourself to attract dark, evil energy into your life and specifically your projects. This might sound superstitious. But be aware. Coke is shit.

Alcohol as a social/personality lubricant

Another way to deny the feelings of awkwardness, shyness and self-consciousness, is to inebriate yourself to varying degrees. This is often combined with cocaine, the combination of which affects a different brain receptor from the two that handle cocaine and alcohol separately, forming a third, conglomerate addiction. Thus the fashion for champagne and cocaine mix.

Alcoholism in varying degrees is increasing in proportion to the increase in general social stress levels.

Red wine in moderation is good for your heart, and the occasional tequila brings on a nice altered state, but as soon as you allow yourself to be socially/emotionally dependent on alcohol/alcohol+cocaine mix, you weaken your aura/energy field/sparkle/shine/charisma factor long-term, as well as your liver and kidneys, *and* talk loads of shit and stumble about inelegantly like a fool.

There are many more effective ways to overcome your social inhibitions, such as speaking your truth honestly, even shyly if needs be, but from your heart, or simply by being extremely kind to people.

It's not that there's anything wrong with alcohol as a frequently employed social lubricant, if you don't mind the strain on your liver/kidneys/self-respect/credibility, premature ageing/bagging of the skin/eyes, etc. For practical purposes, clarity of thought, social grace and morning vitality, most heroes avoid excessive, regular alcohol intake, and prefer instead to explore the realms of their vulnerability in social and public situations. (Or they smoke reefers.)

During phases where alcohol intake is consistently high, take milk thistle herb, as with cocaine, to ease your liver, drink dried-chrysanthemum-flower tea to cool the liver down, eat raw ginger to boost your kidneys, drink extra water, and compensate with extra exercise, especially (intelligently executed) weight-training and other strength/ stamina building techniques.

Taking mind-altering drugs to enhance creativity

Maybe there are eras when it's appropriate and others when it's not. And while it's true that certain judiciously taken hallucinogens and opiates can be effective as creative laxatives/purgatives, if only initially, their use as such these days seems (to me) outmoded and irrelevant, as general levels of awareness increase about meditative methods and other natural mind-altering techniques.

In the latter part of the nineteen hundreds, the use of natural/artificial psychotropic substances, LSD, MDMA, DMT, ketamine, opiates, mescalin, peyote, Iahuassca, 2CB etc., became widespread. In particular, LSD had huge effects on the prevailing culture, still detectable in the popular music and graphic design of today, and was used extensively as a creative purgative, i.e. that which would blast your creative channels open. MDMA on a mass scale rekindled the idea that it's safe to love each other and ourselves.

These days, drugs are boring.

It's almost impossible to get pure MDMA any more. Es are cut with all kinds of crap and do essentially nothing but provide a quick, cheap thrill and make your eyes bulge. The acid you get nowadays doesn't pack the same punch and people don't have time to be wasted for two days at a time anyway, and no one's come up with anything new that's any good for ages (at the time of writing, to the author's limited and unresearched knowledge), which is why the whole club/dance/pills scene is starting to go a bit flat.

As soon as someone does come through with something new, though, there will be another cultural revolution, which will probably be extreme-ly weird and exciting, kill a few people, get lots of press, affect music and graphic design for a while, then be absorbed into the prevailing main-stream culture and die down till the next one comes along.

People/heroes have always used mind-altering substances, especially in the carrying out of creative work, but I'd say it's probably best to stick

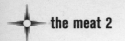

with the odd reefer, what with the way things are going, if you don't want to get caught with your pants down when the *big* changes come.

Importance of developing time-arranging skills

First you need a diary, electronic or manual.

Second you need a watch, clock or other timepiece (sundial etc.).

Third, you need to develop a strong relationship with both, involving regular visual checks on the time and strict adherence to consulting diary pages whenever you make or change an arrangement or wish to block out a chunk of time for working on a project, or going on tour/vacation/ training sessions/retreat/walkabout, etc.

At advanced stages of working with the Five Excellences [see *The Five Excellences* p.121], you may find that you want to split yourself into at least five different parts as the demand for your services and creative offerings increases, and the pressure to deliver to deadline builds up.

As this would spoil your clothes and make a mess on the floor for someone else to clean up, you'll probably find it expedient instead to try the alternative method of effective time arrangement (ETA).

Having assimilated the rudimentary aspects of timepiece/diary-page awareness systems, you must proclaim, 'I am master/mistress of my own time!' Say this over and over until you believe it. Next, decide how much (honestly/realistically/and-don't-underestimate-it) time you need to spend on a particular project. This could be one solid chunk of days/ weeks/months, or a series of such chunks, interspersed with chunks devoted to other projects/activities. It could be a small half-hourly chunk on a daily basis. It could be one day devoted to one project, one day free, next day devoted to another project, and the next for training or whatever. (I mean, I don't know what you get up to, do I?!) But you get my drift.

You can chunk your time into any length you like, according to whatever deadlines have been determined and also what time you need for other projects including the maintenance of your spiritual/emotional/ physical/financial/intellectual/sexual selves. Now all you have to do is write the information into your diary pages and consult those pages whenever making or changing arrangements.

And check your watch regularly and frequently enough, taking readings of the hour and calendar day when necessary, to coordinate your movements accordingly.

Being punctual

Any pro'll tell you. Being punctual is the first sign of being professional. Conversely, as any pro'll also tell you, being late is the first sign you're an amateur, and amateurs don't get the f'n'f. So if you want to be considered a pro enough for people to take you seriously enough to back your projects, *be on time!*

When you're late and keep someone waiting, you're robbing them of time and therefore owe them, which is like getting a detention after school. Lateness, other than when entirely unavoidable, immediately makes you look flaky and unreliable. Psycho-emotionally, you're probably still rebelling against being woken up for school and coerced into following the school agenda.

Say like a mantra, a chant repeated over and over to yourself until it forms a pattern on the wallpaper of your mind, 'I'm always in the right place at the right time!'

But if you want that to be the case, you have to turn up on time. Take a vow to yourself to do so from now on. Say, 'I vow to turn up on time every time from now on, except when my person is unavoidably detained by obstructive solid-matter or people, in which case I vow to make telephonic contact as soon as is heroically possible.'

Doing one thing at a time in rapid succession

When your message/product/self takes off commercially and demand for you is high, your days will often be filled with thirty-one or more important tasks to be accomplished.

Remain completely focused on what you're doing, your mind empty of all other considerations. Then do the next thing you have to do likewise, not thinking of what comes next, and so on, in rapid succession.

Resist the urge to panic. Breathe instead! While doing one thing do not distract yourself by thinking of something else. Keep your attentions unified and focused on one thing at a time. Always be sure to relax and find the most comfortable position under the prevailing circumstances in

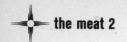

which to place your body, while remaining alert, calm and cheerful (within reason) at all times.

To prevent panic setting in, prioritise. Choose the most pressing task at any moment and start with that, then move on to the next most pressing and so on [see *Making decisions – pendulums, Tarot, I Ching* p.61]. Keep adjusting your priorities as you go along. In this way, your day becomes a meditational process [see *Meditation* p.126] and energy-wastage levels are minimal.

As well as applying to task-accomplishment, this applies equally to the necessary role and costume changes you must make in a day's work in the living theatre of your life [see *Living theatre* p.40].

It in no way implies, however, that you should in any way become robotic. If the situation permits and you feel the urge suddenly to burst forth into song or an impromptu round of break-dancing, for example, simply move that to the top of your priority pile, and as soon as you're done, away you go!

The main thing is to keep breathing and stay with the storyline, while remembering that it's you yourself who have devised said line [see *Fictionalising your life* p.25], and must therefore remember to enjoy it too.

Developing patience, flexibility and humour

Don't wait around for things/phone calls/f'n'f to happen. Carry on with your life. While doing so, develop patience to allow events to unfold each according to its particular Tao.

Develop flexibility (of body and mind) so you can roll with things when they turn out differently to your expectations.

Develop humour so you can laugh your head off while trying to get to sleep, wrapped in old winter newsprint, in your damp cardboard box under a bridge, thinking about how differently it all turned out from how you imagined it would, and wondering what it was that made you buy this book which led you up the garden path like that in the first place.

Impossibility of mastery

Mastering yourself (your fears, foibles and blocking mechanisms) in any field of endeavour, i.e. mastering any art form, is entirely impossible.

There are too many internal factors in a state of flux at any one time, however subtle that flux might be, for you to maintain a consistent state of mastery, however well practised in that particular field of endeavour you may be.

Moreover, any art form you choose to set about mastering has too many inherent aspects for your to pay equal attention to all. Thus, for example, in the practice of Tai Chi [see *The magnificence of Tai Chi* p.144], you'll be flying like a bird through most of the moves and then for no apparent reason one particular posture will threaten to fall apart. You sort that one out and a different one goes. Or you glide like a dancing wu li master through all the moves, but you lose it on the self-defence aspect.

It's like sometimes your brush technique is superb but your colours are a bit off. You get the colour situation rectified and you lose it on the brush strokes.

Mastery is a subjective experience you enjoy more or less fleetingly, from time to time, as you go through the moves of your particular art form, and is in any case relative to the stage of development you've just grown out of.

Any art form you practice, whether it's manipulating the sound of two vinyl discs on a pair of decks or Ikebana flower arranging, provides an infinite number of opportunities for you to develop your skills but in reality can never be fully, permanently mastered, i.e. you can never fully, permanently master yourself in the practice of that art form, however frequently or diligently you practice.

There is nothing negative about this. To think otherwise would simply be arrogant and foolish.

Other people, on seeing you perform flawlessly or produce a so-called masterpiece, may either think you're a master/mistress, or project a master/mistress fantasy on to you, but that's their business. And if they call you master/mistress to your face, you don't have to deny it, it's just that you know better [see *Saying thank you gracefully* p.104].

This should not, in any way, deter you from attempting to master any art form you have an interest in; on the contrary, it's the very impossibility of mastering a particular form that keeps you hooked in to practising it to at least the stage where others think you're a master/mistress, which

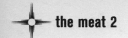

often coincides with them buying your message/produce/services and talking about you in significant numbers thus sending fame and fortune your way.

That notwithstanding, it is now time to look at the Five Excellences and the process of attaining mastery thereof, so you can ascertain for yourself whether they might be of any practical use in helping you shape your path along new, improved, creativity-enhanced lines by next Xmas.

the
juice

THE FIVE EXCELLENCES

A few thousand years ago, an old Taoist, a philosopher by trade, whose name may well have been Loong Shun Po, no one remembers, was lazing around in bed one day, when all of a sudden, in a blinding flash of super-human inspiration, he dreamed up a revolutionary new systematic approach to attaining fame and fortune, consisting of following a fivefold creative path, based on the five elements, the practice of which in time would bring health, wealth and happiness.

The very next day, Loong Shun Po, as we will call him, was sitting in his kitchen drinking soup, bristling with zeal for promoting his new idea, and pondering on what to call it, when a knock came on the door.

It was his good friend Man Lee Kwok, the Buddhist playwright, who had come to borrow some lard. On hearing of Po's fivefold creative path, he clapped his hands together with joy and exclaimed, 'That's excellent!' Loong Shun Po looked up from his soup. 'What was that?' he is reputed to have asked. 'What?' asked Kwok. 'What did you call my fivefold path?' 'Excellent,' replied his puzzled friend.

Po sat for a moment in silence, turning phrases over in his mind: excellent fivefold path, fivefold excellent path, the five …

'Eureka!' cried Po suddenly, in Chinese. 'The Five Excellences! That's it! Henceforth, this path shall be called the path of the Five Excellences!'

And thus the system was born. It was slow to catch on at first, however, on account of a general paucity of marketing, promotion and communica-tion systems (Digital TV/Internet, etc.) at that time, as well as a prevailing fashion for only eight and tenfold path systems, and it was not until many millennia later, during which Taoism underwent many permutations before returning to its original Wayward form, that the Five Excellences resurfaced in North London of all places and was faithfully reformulated and repackaged as *Handbook for Heroes*, by Barefoot Doctor.

You like that shit?!

The concept of being master of the Five Excellences is actually more likely to have arisen some time after Confucius (Kung Fu Tse) as a result of philosophical fusion between Taoist, Buddhist and Confucianist schools of thought.

In fact, the Five Excellences is merely the name of a concept, which is that if you master the five separate strands of meditation, martial arts, healing, composition and presentation, you'll always be able to trade one or more of your skills for food and lodging at least, and will, if you carry things out just so, stand to make a considerable fortune and gain great fame.

Calling someone master/mistress of the Five Excellences is the highest accolade.

Worst-case scenario

The world as you know it comes to an end. Through general infrastructural breakdown, economic collapse, sudden social structure disintegration, war, disease, famine, catastrophic weather conditions, flooding, burning, ecological meltdown, earthquake, volcano, or just plain old planetary cataclysm, you find yourself one day, far from the city, far from the suburbs, holed up in a cave on a mountainside with a few other survivors.

Being a master/mistress of the Five Excellences, however, you find your position is relatively strong in as far as your survival may depend on your companions.

By meditating you can calm yourself, recharge yourself, and deal better with your existential crisis and that of others in relation to adjusting to your new conditions.

By practising martial arts, you maintain your physical safety self-confidence levels, in relation to defending yourself from someone attacking you manually for your biscuit ration. You keep yourself fit, agile and healthy. And you can teach the others who are bound to be impressed and say things like, 'I've always wanted to learn Tai Chi, and what with the world having come to an end and us being thrown together like this, I wondered whether you might be interested in trading me lessons for a vest made of mountain grass and a hot pine-cone stew.' And so your survival would be secured a while longer.

Practising healing arts means you can help save, preserve and ameliorate the lives of your fellow survivors, and thus, once your skills have been proven, ensure for yourself a privileged place in the queue for food (pine-cone stew, fried tick, etc.), and reduce the chances of someone attempting to assault your person with intent to maim or take life unless, or course, you're messing with their lover. Moreover, you can do self-healing to help maintain your own strength, balance and health, and teach your healing arts to your companions so they can do so too, which will not diminish the demand for *your* services and thereby reduce your safety levels, but will actually increase your standing on account of the respect you engender.

If that doesn't do the trick and they're threatening to evict you from the cave for not being useful enough by the next full moon, which you calculate to be in only one week's time, don't despair. Because you practice the art of composing, you set to work immediately on the composition of a farce, the central theme of which is to cast your current situation in a humorous light. You compose the storyline, script. You write the music, you conceive the look of the thing, you come up with a name, and devise a marketing strategy, i.e. a way to entice them into wanting to 'pay' (with bits of bone/stone/food/clothing/services, etc.) to watch the show.

Then, because you also practice the arts of presentation, you manage, through a series of huge, improvisational, creative compromises, to produce the show, carve the flyers on bits of rock, promote it properly well in time for the full moon, get a full house, rave reviews and secure your place in the cave for another month.

Obviously the efficacy of the system is not restricted to worst-case, post-world-end scenarios. Quite the opposite, in fact, because the less worst-case the scenario gets, the more effectively your mastery of the Five Excellences takes care of you.

At the other extreme, in a world of peace and plenty (chance would be a fine thing), the punters get bored and, after they've exhausted the momentary pleasures of shopping and fucking, start yearning for something a little deeper, something a little more spiritual (sir/madam?). So they turn to you, with your tranquil air and calm demeanour, to teach them meditation and to write books about it, etc.

And as the ennui spreads and deepens and the need for spiritual sustenance increases beyond the point where simply meditating is no longer

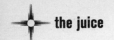

enough to quell the restlessness, people start turning to exploring the connection between body, mind and spirit in the mysterious practice of martial arts. And you'll be there to teach them. And in this world of peace and plenty (and I repeat, chance would be a fine thing), because they've nothing more dangerous to worry about but still have daily worry quotas, ingrained from millions of years of survival conditioning, to fill, they start worrying about their health, their stress levels, their allergies, their childhoods, etc. So who do they come to? You, the healer.

With things being so good, there's a surplus of cash floating about (yerright!), and people are desperate to invest in anything, and they're falling over themselves to throw money at the creative offerings you have composed.

Because things are so easy and abundant, you can afford to spend the time on the details of presentation, promotion, marketing and distribution, and your offering gets taken up with relish by an eager market place, and you end up being a multi-billionaire.

In practice, the Five Excellences system works everywhere in between those two extremes.

The Five Elements and the Five Excellences

The Five Elements according to both Traditional and Wayward Taoist Schools, are:

Water, the life-giving/supporting (as in the sea)

Wood, the upward and outward pushing movement; progress, growth, expansion (as in trees)

Fire, The light, heat, and passion (as in the sun/other stars)

Earth, the sustaining/nourishing (as in a planet on which to fulfil your marketing ambitions and grow your food in the ground thereof)

Metal/Air, the incisive, decisive, discriminatory (as in blades cutting through, as in spiritual intelligence/ability to see things from the air/sky)

The Five Elements are mutually supportive, as in one feeds, sustains or enables the next. Water enables the trees to grow. Trees provide wood to burn in the Fire. Fire makes ashes (Earth). The sun (ultimate Fire) makes planets (Earth). Earth provides Metals. Metal provides the material for buckets to carry Water, and so on.

The Five Elements also contain and potentially destroy each other. Water stops the Fire getting too hot. The Fire condenses the Water to stop it overflowing. Metal cuts through Wood to stop it growing unwieldy. Wood blunts Metal to stop it getting too sharp for its own good. I could go on, but you get the picture, and I suggest you explore the connections for yourself.

The balance of power between the five is constantly shifting, within your body, where each element corresponds with a different organ and bowel, in your psyche, where each element corresponds to a different mood or emotion, and in the world around you, where the hours, days, seasons, years, directions and even get-rich-and-famous schemes find their correspondences in the Five Elements.

In respect of the Five Excellences:

Earth corresponds with meditation, as in sustaining yourself by sitting on the floor and being still
Metal corresponds with martial arts, as in slicing someone's bollocks off with a sword (in self-defence, of course!)
Water corresponds with healing, as in supporting life and enabling life force to flow
Wood corresponds with composition, as in an idea growing, taking shape and spreading out (like a tree)
Fire corresponds with presentation, as in the bright light and flame of fame, i.e. glare of the footlights/spotlights/flashlights, as you present your project to the world.

According to the formula, meditation gives you the sense to take up (and keep up) martial arts. (Earth supporting Metal.) Martial arts give you the self-confidence and chi (energy) to heal/deal with people. (Metal supporting Water.) Healing earns you money to support yourself while you compose your symphony/book/movie/whatever project. (Water supporting Wood.) Your compositional skills give you a product to which to apply your presentation skills in presenting/promoting/marketing it.

(Wood supporting Fire.) Presenting your work effectively earns you the money to buy the house you need (Earth) to do your meditation in.

Conversely, too much meditation means not enough composition time (empty field – Earth with no trees/wood).

So you stay mindful of the mix at any time and can thus help effect a balance between the five phases of activity.

It may not have any practical value to know this, but it helps you to inculcate the system into your own. And moreover, it's neat! (If you're in the mood.)

EXCELLENCE – NUMBER ONE: MEDITATION (EARTH ELEMENT)

The purpose of meditation is to empty your mind of thoughts in order to give it a rest so it can self-rejuvenate/recharge and thus be more relaxed, alert and effective in controlling your actions, words and thoughts, and thus enable you to be more at peace with yourself at all times no matter what activity/thought process you may be involved in.

Moreover, keeping your mind filled up with thoughts at all times leaves little room for new information to have the deep impact it often deserves. It is like pouring tea into a cup which is already full. It just spills over the sides. This is especially true for creative information seeking to find expression through you [see *Discovering and following your Muse* p.172]. Creative information requires space in which to sit so you can see it properly. When the mind is full of thought, creativity gets lost amongst the clutter.

Just like with most bowels, it is healthiest to empty most minds at least once a day, preferably in the morning before starting work.

To do this, simply sit comfortably and think of nothing for half an hour. For long-lasting results, repeat that procedure every day for the rest of your life. You may, however, find this difficult. The majority do. Always have, in fact. Which is why the wise old eastern people of yore developed various methods to help keep the mind focused on nothing.

There are countless schools of meditation from all the various spiritual disciplines around the world, ancient and modern. All, however, have the same root purpose: emptying the mind of chatter so it can rest instead in the magnificent stillness of universal consciousness/ Tao long enough to get you back on full charge.

The Taoists developed a no-nonsense, straightahead approach, drawing a series of maps/charts of the interior 'structure' of the psyche otherwise known as the psychic-body or spirit-body. Taking into account how our minds like to dart about like monkeys in a tree from one thought to another, they found ways to split their attention, so that one part is 'fixed' in the centre of the brain, another is moving slowly around the psycho-physical body in pre-set patterns, another is on the breath (rhythm, smoothness and depth), another is on the physical posture, another is watching for errant thoughts, another is visualising certain symbols or images, and yet another is listening for the kettle to boil so they can make a cup of tea.

It's a bit like spinning plates on sticks. There's always something more for your monkey mind to focus on, until it cancels itself out. Ah, and then the peace. What the clever bastards in fact developed was a system of internal alchemy so sophisticated in its power to alter your consciousness and physiological state, that regular daily practice gives you the power of superman/woman, and if you don't believe me, look up in the sky.

What follows is a sequence of meditational/alchemical processes for you to experiment with on your own. The sequence starts with the basic meditational template, and progresses on to processes specifically related to creativity enhancement and fame and fortune attainment.

But first:

The meaninglessness of deep daily meditation

Deep daily meditation practice reveals that things only have the meaning you give them. This is true for all phenomena in your life including your- self, other people and all the events that occur involving same.

Phenomena arise of themselves out of nowhere (the Tao) and return thence likewise. Simply observe serenely without giving them meaning or seeking for meaning in them.

This is the meaninglessness you experience with daily meditational practice, and though it may sound frighteningly psychologically anarchic, and could indeed induce psychotic episodes among readers with less psychic hardiness/foolhardiness [see *Disclaimer and polite warning* p.5], it usually works a treat for easing mental stress and releasing you from self-limiting narrow-mindedness, and hence encouraging lateral mentation processes whence springs original creativity.

To reinforce this idea, for no more than seven minutes every hour for the next four hours, notice everything your eyes fall upon, including the thoughts in your inner-land/mind-scape, and say, 'I have given this the meaning it has for me', as in, I have given this situation the meaning it has for me, I have given this turtle the meaning it has for me, etc.

Sitting comfortably to meditate

You can meditate in any position you like, but unless otherwise physically restricted from doing so, sitting comfortably in a quiet space with your eyes closed is the most convenient for regular daily practice. With experience you can meditate in a headstand, handstand, walking, running, upright-standing, lying down and even hopping, skipping and jumping if the mood should so take you.

For now, sit on the floor or in a chair, back supported if necessary, and make your spine be perpendicular to the ground, that is neither leaning to left or right, nor inclining forwards or backwards but straight up and down. Then make your head be set straight on your shoulders likewise.

Imagine you have a golden thread attached at one end to the crown of your head and at the other to the ceiling/heaven/sky/sky-lab, which is pulling upwards and thus lengthening your spine (gently).

Simultaneously imagine your shoulders are each moving out to the sides away from each other, and your hip/sitting bones likewise, so that it feels as if your torso is broadening and lengthening at the same time.

Fundamentals: Breathing

Does your belly appear to expand like a balloon as you inhale and contract again as you exhale, while your chest remains relatively stable?

Is your breathing slow and of even tempo?

Are your in-breaths and out-breaths of equal duration?

Is your breath silent and smooth like fine silk?

If your answer is no to any of these, reverse what you're doing,

So:

When you inhale keep your chest still and let your belly expand like a balloon.

When you exhale keep your chest still and let your belly contract again.

Slow your breath down and make each inhalation-exhalation cycle of even tempo.

Make your in-breath and out-breath of equal duration.

Make your breath silent and smooth like fine silk.

Practice these breath manoeuvres whenever and wherever you can, until they become automatic and constant.

As well as for meditating, you can then use correct, full diaphragm breathing, as a helpful adjunct to many other gentle activities including driving, cycling, dishwashing, sex-doing, money-counting, applause-receiving, hairdressing, haberdashery and almost anything else you care to mention.

Fundamentals: Relaxing/Sinking

Check your body for muscular stress.

In the sitting position, necessary tension is the minimum required to stop your head from rolling or your body from falling over. Anything excess to this is muscular stress, which not only impedes meditational practice but greatly reduces health and overall effectiveness in general while simultaneously triggering mental stress and in more severe cases causing death.

Release any unnecessary tension from your musculature. Imagine all muscular tension melting and dripping downwards through your body like treacle on to the floor.

Trusting your skeleton to hold you upright [see *Sitting comfortably to meditate* p.128], allow yourself to sink in the direction of the Earth's centre.

Fundamentals: Say hello to your mind

To do this, think about one point in the centre of your brain and allow your awareness to gather itself together there. From now on, observe everything from this point. (With practice this can and should be used

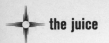

with eyes open during the performance of all normal and abnormal daily activity.)

You will probably become quickly aware of intensive thought activity (ITA) occurring in the forebrain, situated directly in front of your central-brain observation point. By observing ITA as a visual pattern of swirling thoughtforms rather than succumbing to temptations to follow/explore any particular thoughtform and thus get lost in a thoughtstream, you will notice ITA gradually decreasing until it slows to a trickle and then, on a good day, to nothing.

At first this experience of thinking about nothing will only last for a few brief moments at a time, but with regular practice you'll be able to extend those moments indefinitely.

Fundamentals: Connect to your 'tan tien'

To prevent yourself falling asleep or otherwise drifting off ether-bound, anchor yourself to physical waking awareness by establishing a firm and constant mental connection with your 'tan tien', a point two thumb-widths down and in from your belly-button. Tan tien means field of heaven, i.e. spiritual-energy connecting point. Constant awareness of and mental connection to it, gives validity and authenticity to all your actions/deeds/ words, and is an essential tenet of martial arts practice [see *Martial arts* p.138]. Practising it while sitting is the most effective way of learning to make friends with it, and will stop your mind wandering while you meditate.

Once your mental connection with the centre-brain observation point is firmly established, i.e. you find yourself comfortably observing your inner-landscape from there, simultaneously think about the one point of the 'tan tien'.

Holding awareness in centre-brain while simultaneously thinking about your 'tan tien', causes a connection between the two, so that they appear and feel one and the same.

Now you're flying.

Hardcore practice

For the following advanced/hardcore techniques, relating specifically to the enhancement of creativity and acceleration of your fame and fortune attainment programme (FAFAP), you'd be well advised to practise the above fundamentals to a stage where you can hold steady, thinking about (practically) nothing for at least two minutes, thirty-seven seconds at a time, otherwise the addition of extra information will induce instant high levels of jumble factor.

Hardcore practice: Secret (no longer) Taoist energy control and visualisation mechanism for enhancing creativity

Having attended to fundamentals and managed to maintain a relatively stable thinking-about-(practically)-nothing status for the duration of (approximately) thirty-six breath cycles, follow this exercise if you wish to open your creative channels and/or increase the volume, clarity and general quality of creative impulses coming through you:

Visualise a channel/psychic tube (Creation Channel) running from the inside of the centre of your forehead, backwards over the top of your brain to the inside of the centre of the base of your skull.

As you breathe in, imagine/feel the breath is entering through the centre of your forehead in the front and passing along the channel/psychic tube to the base of your skull at the back.

As you breathe out, imagine/feel the breath reverse and pass back along the channel/psychic tube to the front again.

With every back-and-forth-breath pass you make, imagine/feel that the central

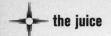

(mid) line running over the top of your head is becoming progressively wider. This gives the effect of your head splitting in two, but in a nice way. As your head splits wider and wider in two it creates the further effect of your brain/receptive consciousness growing more available to incoming (cosmic) information, i.e. creative impulses. In other words, it opens up the top of your head to allow the creativity through. Now just sit in that state for as long as it lasts or as long as you've got.

The sensation engendered after only four or five passes can be exciting. Avoid becoming distracted by that excitement, with thoughts such as 'isn't this exciting'. Avoid forgetting, i.e. remember to maintain your observation post in the centre of your brain and its connection to your 'tan tien', maintain maximum relaxation/sinking levels, maintain regulated breathing patterns, and maintain upright posture throughout the procedure.

If high levels of jumble factor should occur, *bring your mind back immediately to the breath* and start again.

You can further increase the effectiveness of this creativity-booster if you imagine your breath is coloured a purple-gold mix and moves like light through the psychic tube; visualise a stream of creative impulses, carrying the information you need for your projects, originating from far out in space, and landing on your bonce (penetrating your consciousness); feel yourself receiving and absorbing this information in its raw/uncarved form.

Do not attempt to examine, analyse, categorise or organise this stream into usable shape, or you'll stop the flow (with your busy mind). Simply receive [see *Developing receptivity* p.94]. The results will become readily apparent in the hours/days/weeks/months that follow.

To return to normal consciousness, simply reverse the procedure without reclaiming any former stress on the way out if possible.

Practice this at least once every nine days for an ongoing effect, and every day if you're in a hurry.

Hardcore practice: Secret (no longer) Taoist energy control and visualisation mechanism for generating fame

Same attention to fundamentals as above required, after which, visualise a channel/psychic tube running from a point right between your legs (perineum) immediately in front of your anus and behind your genitals, upwards to your 'tan tien', two thumb widths (approximately!) in and down from your navel.

As you breathe in, imagine/feel your breath enter through your perineum and travel upwards through the psychic tube to your 'tan tien'.

As you breathe out, imagine/feel your breath travelling back down the tube and out again through your perineum.

Repeated between nine and thirty-six times, this will (energetically) 'open' your belly in the same way as the previous technique opens your head. The lower abdomen is your psychic-body's reception area for the incoming energy of other people, which can be and often is negative/ destructive. Which is why *it is dangerous to practise this without the addition of the following:*

On the inhalation, imagine/visualise/feel that you're magnetising/drawing towards you a stream of energy lit in bright (positive) golden-white light, originating from the chests, i.e. heart-centres (if you want to be specific) of everyone *on the planet. Inhale that mixture (all psychic negative-content now neutralised) all the way up to your 'tan tien'.*

On exhalation, see/imagine-you-see/feel your breath professionally lit in black (UV) light, passing back down the psychic tube to your perineum, thence emitting forth into the world, enabling you to see everyone's psychic dandruff/ teeth/eyeballs. This black light acts like a vacuum which attracts the bright, golden-white light of public acknowledgement/adulation unto itself.

Polite warning: this is a dangerous technique [see *Disclaimer and polite warning* p.5] because it works. It is recommended to read up on psychic shielding methods in *Handbook For The Urban Warrior*, before putting yourself at risk and/or consult your doctor. This mechanism should be reactivated on a daily or bi-daily basis for best results. Results will be evident in two to three months.

Hardcore practice: Secret (no longer) Taoist energy control and visualisation mechanism for generating fortune

Visualise a channel/psychic tube starting in the centre of your forehead and running down the front of your body to your 'tan tien', the point two thumb-widths in and down from your umbilicus. Visualise the 'tan tien' as a gateway to a vast inner chamber psycho-physically located in your lower abdomen.

On inhalation, see/imagine/feel the breath enter the psychic tube through your forehead and pass downwards to your 'tan tien'.

On exhalation, see/imagine/feel the breath enter the inner chamber in your belly.

Visualise the in-breath, lit strongly in bright gold, carrying with it a stream of wealth in whatever form best represents the idea of wealth to you. This may be diamonds and rubies and other assorted treasures or wads of high denomination banknotes, bank drafts or cheques. (Do not accept credit cards as they take up to two and a half per cent commission.)

On the out-breath, visualise this stream of wealth entering the inner chamber from your 'tan tien'.

Repeat this procedure until the inner chamber is full. This mechanism should be reactivated on a daily or bi-daily basis for best results.

Warning: sudden physical movement may cause belly to rattle.

Hardcore practice: Secret (no longer) Taoist energy control and visualisation mechanism for generating charisma

Visualise a channel/psychic tube beginning at the centre of your chest and running down the inside of your body to your 'tan tien', two thumb-widths in and down from your navel.

As you breathe in, see/imagine/feel the breath entering your body through the centre of your chest and travelling downwards through the psychic tube to your 'tan tien'.

As you breathe out, see the breath travel upwards along the tube and out again through the centre of your chest. Once out of your chest, see it radiate from you in ever-exponentially-expanding circles around you, i.e. every time you breathe out the circles get bigger.

Light up the in-breath in deep crimson, and visualise that it carries a stream of life-sustaining power into your 'tan tien'.

Light up the out-breath in strong golden-pinky rose and, as it emits forth from your chest, watch it become more intense the further out it spreads from your body.

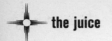

This golden-pinky-rose light represents the energetic substance of charisma, and the deep crimson, the life-sustaining power necessary to support you when you're engaged in strong giving-outwards activity [see *Developing generosity* p.96].

This mechanism should be reactivated at least once a day, with extra reactivations recommended before social/professional events/appearances of any kind. As well as being a meditational device, this mechanism can be played with to interesting effect while otherwise engaged in social/professional activities in the external world. Regular daily practice for ninety days (no credit) will not only increase your charisma levels noticeably enough for people to remark on it, but will moreover increase inner-peace-factor levels significantly, as a pleasant by-product.

Hardcore technique: Placing the star-symbol

The Doctor's star-symbol, which the author was 'given' eighteen years ago at a bizarre ceremony in northern New Mexico, by Machwalla, a big

player in the holy-man stakes, is a magical talisman. It is representative of a star, the star Sirius (8.6 light years from the sun), whence ancient tribes, all around the globe, believed came (extraterrestrial) visitors on more than one occasion in the course of human history, either in physical or psychic/telepathic form to inform our human intelligences, in order that we/they might grow in some way, but to what end, I haven't a clue. Whether the above-mentioned ceremony did indeed cause an infusion of 'Sirius-energy', as was intended, or whether that's just bunkum, my experiments with the symbol as a meditative/healing tool/aid/amplifier have born great fruit for me and those I have healed, and it behoves me now to share it with you.

Placing the star-symbol works like waving a wand. Wherever you place it, your focus at that place will be intensified/magnified/amplified. All magical operations from all occult systems depend on the mental focus of the operator. Placing your focus on an idea, person or object and your energy/magic power follows. The effects of this will depend on your intention. Placing the star-symbol on an idea, object or person magnifies and intensifies your focus and therefore your energy/magic power for greater impact.

When meditating, place it in your 'tan tien' and it will intensify your life-sustaining power. Place it in the centre of your chest and it will intensify your charisma/love-flow. Place it behind the centre of your forehead and you will intensify your entire being.

Wherever you wish to direct intense focus, place the star-symbol there. It can also be used for healing yourself and others [see *Hardcore technique: Placing the star symbol* p.136].

When visualising something you want, place the symbol over the picture and your visualisation-effectiveness factor will be increased dramatically.

Use the symbol at any point during the meditational practices described above. If I was rationed to delivering one single piece of information which will further you, that would be the one. Obviously the star-symbol can be substituted for any other symbol/icon/motif you like. If you give a symbol power, power it'll have.

EXCELLENCE NUMBER TWO: MARTIAL ARTS (METAL ELEMENT)

Tai Chi, Hsing I and Pa Kua propaganda

I don't know if it's because they're a bunch of pugnacious bastards or if it's because they're very wise, or both, but martial arts (literally, the arts of Mars, god of war), have always played an important role in the cultures of East and South-East Asia. There are hundreds, maybe thousands of styles and sub-styles (schools, philosophies, methods and secrets), but they can be divided into external styles, sometimes known as hard styles, and internal styles, sometimes known as soft.

The external styles, which are by far the majority, focus at the early and intermediate stages on the development of external muscular strength, speed and toughening of the body surfaces by employing methods such as dipping your hand in and out of a bucket of sand, forcefully and rapdily one thousand and eight times. The practice of external styles usually involves the pumping to the body surface of much perspiration and often necessitates sustaining injury to your person. To make progress you have to be hard (all over). Eventually at highly advanced master/ mistress levels your focus becomes internal (to be explained).

The internal arts, which are essentially Taoist (Wayward and otherwise), focus in the early stages of practice on the development of internal strength produced by harnessing mind, breath and chi (energy/cultivated life-force). The cultivation of chi lends the practitioner a superhuman level of personal power which can, after many years' training and instruction, be highly effective for self-defence and for healing (self and others).

Highly cultivated chi (energy) can also be used to support and enhance the inner alchemical-spiritual process involved in the practice of meditation [see *Meditation* p.126]. Only after years of practice can you use the internal arts effectively for self-defence, because you can't rush the chi-cultivation process. It's like a river, and you can't push a river, all you can do is prepare the ground and wait for the water. But finally, after anything from one to twenty years' practice, when that chi does start coming through, and depending on how well all the moves have been practised, you become more or less invincible (in theory). The practice of internal arts is not strenuous, requires no excesses of perspiration and injury-sustaining potential is minimal. In contrast to external styles, to be any good you've got to be soft.

External styles rely on overcoming your opponent with superior strength and speed. Internal styles rely on using your opponent's superior strength and speed rather than your own, i.e. intelligence, to overcome them.

The relatively sweat- and injury-free training methods of the internal styles means that, in reality, it's more likely you'll continue regular training until you die than you would if practising external styles.

This is important, for, though the beneficial effects on your health and psyche become quickly evident after only a few weeks of study, the truly profound master/mistress-level benefits don't kick in till you've paid your dues, i.e. until you're pretty old. If fighting/self-defence is your sole reason for taking up the study of martial arts, and neither inner clarity, inner peace, health, longevity, grace, enlightenment nor superhuman power interests you much, it's better to study Western boxing, which still remains the most effective form of fight-winning self-defence, kickboxing or any of the other external forms that interest you.

If, on the other hand, you want to be one of those heroes who still wants to get all the girls/boys when you're eighty-three, and like the prospect of getting more accomplished, stronger and more powerful the older you get, as well as feeling relaxed, alert, agile, peaceful, self-confident, self-secure, and always have a teaching job to fall back on in your dotage, then the internal styles are for you.

Of these, the most famous are the Taoist arts of Tai Chi, Hsing I and Pa Kua. And as this book is based on the Taoist approach, albeit a little waywardly, and is furthermore describing the Five Excellences, itself a Taoist scheme, and is scribed by a Wayward Taoist, whose martial expertise, such that it is after only thirty years training, is mostly limited to the Taoist martial arts, it's these we're going to examine. (Funnily enough.)

Obviously, it's impossible to learn martial arts adequately from a

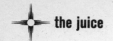

book. You need a real-life teacher. What's presented here is intended onl
to inspire you to take up, continue, or intensify the practice of these art
and to demystify some of the principles involved.

These principles can be adapted for use during any form of exercise (
psycho-physical training and, whether you use the following material i
that way, or are inspired by it to take up, continue or intensify Tai Ch
Hsing I, and/or Pa Kua training, it is important to remember that a her
needs daily exercise to remain in correct functioning mode for the dur;
tion.

The common principles of Tai Chi, Hsing I and Pa Kua

Of the three 'sisters', Hsing I is probably the oldest, and is the one whic
most resembles straightforward boxing/kick-boxing disciplines, thoug
in execution its moves are far more fluid, elegant and explosive. Of th
three, Hsing I gives you combat-preparedness-status the quickes
Indeed, you could be ploughing through the heftiest of opponents wit
devastating effect after only one or two years of dedicated practice. Th
more profound psycho-spiritual benefits, however, do not usually kick i
till a few years later.

Pa Kua is probably the second oldest (exact dates of origin of all thre
are unknown and shrouded in myth and conjecture, but they can b
safely, even conservatively estimated to have originated anywhere fro;
four hundred and eighty to one thousand, one hundred and nine yea;
ago), and resembles Dervishes whirling or, when practised with tw
scythes as it often is, a human rotor-blade fighting machine. Of the thre
its practice engenders the most pronounced and immediate altered stat
of consciousness.

Tai Chi is the youngest of the three and the one which least resem
bles straightforward fighting styles. It is, however, also the mo;
comprehensive, sophisticated and highly evolved of the three, and ult
mately the most powerful for self-defence as well as spiritual/person;
development.

Dedicated practitioners often/usually train extensively in all three on
daily basis (myself, I do, and recommend you do, two hours ever
morning and a little bit at night if you can, outside if possible).

This cross-fertilisation of chi is made both desirable and possible by the convenient fact that all three share and are governed by a set of common fundamental Taoist principles, which comprise the following:

Remain relaxed, mentally throw open all your joints, let your flesh feel soft (not unnecessarily taut), as if you're sinking towards the Earth's centre. Key relaxation focus points are forehead, chest and anus. Never hold your breath, but keep it flowing freely and smoothly. Rough, unregulated breathing leads to rough, anarchic energy.

The crown of your head feels like it's suspended by a golden/silver thread to the top of the sky. Alternatively, it feels as if there is a small ball of bright-glowing light spinning unexpectedly a few inches above the crown of your head. Either way, the top of your head feels light. Traditionally this is called raising the spirit of (positive) vitality to the top of the head, which has the effect of bringing clarity of vision, and positivity/cheerfulness of mind (and is therefore highly recommended to be practised at all times, martial artist or not).

All movement is initiated from the 'tan tien', a psychic energy centre two thumb-widths down and in from your belly button. When your 'tan tien' moves, the rest of your body follows. When it comes to rest again, the body does too.

All parts of the body are coordinated and move as one unit that is so finely balanced that even a ladybug can't land on your arm without setting the whole unit in motion.

You might consider this over-reactive response slightly excessive, but it is this very sensitivity which enables the experienced practitioner instinctively to interpret his/her opponent's energy and thus stay one step ahead of the game. This interpreting of other people's energy is tantamount to having psychic power.

Obviously this martial focus is also useful for business negotiations of any kind. The spirit commands the mind. The mind commands the chi. The chi commands the body and, hopefully, the body commands the superior position in any combative situation.

Chi is stored in the spine, which then issues it like a bow releasing its arrow, through the hands/feet/weapon you're striking with. Always let the chi sink back down into the 'tan tien' region after use, to be restored/regenerated for further use.

Your shoulders correspond with your hips, your knees correspond with your

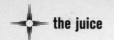
the juice

elbows, ankles with wrists, feet with hands, and nose with navel. Hence, yo
shoulders move to be in line with your hips. Your punch doesn't extend past
toes of your front foot. Your nose remains in line with your navel, and yo
navel remains in line with your mind.

Defeat an oncoming force of a thousand pounds with only four ounces
strength. Imagine a nuclear-tipped missile coming at your head. Just before
point of impact, you turn your head, i.e. yield just enough and no more for it
miss you, whereupon it crashes into the country further on, saving you
experience of sudden, unwanted head-removal and extreme radiation poisoni
That's four ounces defeating a force of a thousand pounds. The other, more t
ditional analogy is that of pulling a thousand-pound bull by a chain through
nose with only four ounces worth of tug. When receiving a thousand-pound bl
to the body, you soften, empty and turn so that the thousand-pound force fir
no surface to land on with more than four ounces of weight.

You focus your intention through rather than simply on the target you w
to hit. Your intention issues forth from the centre of your forehead (yer toyd ey
and once released is unstoppable.

In defending against attack, you neutralise/counter-attack, inflicting
absolute minimum of damage to achieve your goal (of not being attacked age
in the immediately upcoming future by the person you've just neutralised/cou
tered).

Always distinguish between full and empty.

When your opponent attacks your right side, you yield (further to the righ
thus emptying your right and filling your left which has simultaneously swu
round (also to the right) and thus clobbered your opponent's right side.

This clobbering is called sticking to your opponent, as in when he/she attac
you yield so that however far he/she advances, he/she never reaches you, and
when retreating from you he/she can never get away, because you're stuck
him/her like superglue.

If your opponent doesn't attack your right side, however, do nothing.

Always wait for your opponent to make the first move and then get th
ahead of him/her, i.e. follow your opponent but get there first.

Embrace your opponent with love.

If given the chance, tickling your opponent into submission is preferable
gouging his/her eyes out.

Match your opponent's speed of movement. Never set the pace. If your oppo-
nt attacks fast, defend/counter/respond fast.

Always compliment your opponent whenever possible, as in 'great biceps!', or
ce punch!' Not only do you open the possibility for a new friendship to
elop, but also cause his/her chi to rise upwards with vain pride, thus making
m energetically top-heavy and therefore easier to topple.

If you're facing off against a really big guy/gal in a life/death situation, the
t place to aim for is the throat/windpipe, not the balls (especially with women)
ball-strikes often have a delayed reaction whereas a quick, hard, well-placed
ing I 'drilling' punch to the throat, for example, will always do the trick. Pay
ention before responding thus, however, as execution of this move can easily
ult in simultaneous execution of your opponent, and subsequent incarcera-
n/execution of yourself.

For this reason always keep your chin down to protect your throat. A down-
rdly directed chin also has the effect of lengthening the back of your neck,
ich goes along with the suspended head principle.

Avoid being double-weighted on your feet, i.e. having your weight evenly dis-
buted between your two feet, except at the start and end of the forms. Always
at least 60/40, 70/30, 100/0, front/back or back/front, and keep shifting regu-
ly.

Do not try to attack/counter-attack from a distance, with a long roundhouse
k, for example, but always attempt to gain entry into your opponent's per-
ual space, i.e. within the scope of his/her embrace. This is known as inside
hting.

Avoid high kicks, both coming at you, and coming from you, as these are
ier to ward off than low ones which often slip your opponent's notice. Most of
time, confine your kicks to your opponent's knees and below, i.e. destroy the
ndations and the building topples.

Always attempt to negotiate verbally before resorting to fisticuffs.

Always take the turn-and-run option whenever expedient [see Let them call
u pisher, p.101].

The spirit is perfectly calm in the midst of movement/danger.

Remain upright, leaning neither too far forwards or backwards, nor to the left
d right. In this way, the spinal column, which is the central most important
rgy channel in the body, is more able to distribute chi evenly round the body.

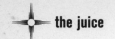

Store energy in your navel.

Distinguish hard from soft. Soft response is always better than a hard one.

Remain calm and centred at all times. Only look in your opponent's e
when already fully committed to the (counter-) attack, and wish to overco
him/her psychically. Otherwise keep your gaze fixed in the mid-air space betwe
your two chests, whence you can observe all peripheral hand and foot movemer
of your opponent, however big or small, without moving your eyes. This also p
vents you becoming hypnotised/overcome by your opponent's psychic for
which is easily released through the eyes (all three).

Most of these principles form a by-no-means-comprehensive list, bu
could go on all day/night, and can be readily adapted to activities in norm
civilian life and also to other styles of martial arts and exercise systems.

The magnificence of Tai Chi

Serious Tai Chi players (you should lighten up), must forgive the oc
sional extreme irreverence displayed herein. Having been a dedicate
diligent Tai Chi student, teacher and practitioner myself now for ov
twenty years, I feel I've earned the right.

You can be a complete dickhead, your mind sunk in the soup of yo
various delusions, insecurities casting a confusing glow over yo
thoughts, but do some Tai Chi and for twenty minutes or so, you feel li
a hero of superhuman ability, skill and strength, dancing with the cr
ative power of the Tao itself. Then you stop and within moments you'
just the same prat/geek you were before.

That's the magnificence of Tai Chi.

Of course, over time, the effects on your inner being accumulate a
eventually, on reaching and bursting through critical mass levels, t
experience of mastery/mistressry you experience in your Tai Chi sessio
extends for longer and longer into your day, until you start to feel th
way, fairly unwaveringly, most of the time.

Tai Chi Chuan, as is its full moniker, means boxing method f
accessing supreme ultimate reality, and with good reason, though it c
tainly doesn't *look* like boxing at first glance.

When you see someone in the early morning park slowly waving th
arms around and making pretty patterns in the air, what they're actua

doing is performing an extended series of boxing/self-defence poses linked together smoothly in slow motion to form one long continuous stream of intensely refined and graceful movement.

This is the solo shadow-boxing form, which is mostly practised at approximately one third of the speed of 'normal' human movement, to give your mind time to track on to a series of key focus points (to be explained shortly), to appreciate and savour fully the profound pleasure of experiencing the unification of body, mind, spirit and energy, and to feel that chi (energy) whooshing through your system like a tidal wave.

During the performance of the solo form, which lasts approximately for the duration of the burning of one ten-gramme good quality blond incense stick (fifteen minutes) and is thus called the long form, you are in a state of deep meditation-in-movement throughout, and feel like you're flying, gliding or swimming through the air, while simultaneously feeling rooted to the power coming up from the Earth's centre. That's known in the business as connecting Heaven and Earth.

Daily practice of the long form is supplemented by a series of highly effective back-up training exercises which are designed to increase strength, stamina, flexibility, balance, agility, speed, mobility of the joints, reduce aches and pains, boost immune response, clear the mind, increase focusing and concentration power, increase general energy levels, activate 'super-charged' chi (energy) flow, hone your striking/ kicking skills, improve your footwork and generally loosen you up to enjoy practising the form more.

There are many schools of Tai Chi, the most well known of which are those of the Chen family, the Yang (nothing to do with yin and yang), and the Wu (pronounced 'woooo' and said in a very high-pitched voice). All three schools follow more or less the same sequence of poses in the long form, but with subtle and sometimes dramatic stylistic differences in the execution of individual postures, in the long form and in the warm-up/back-up/support exercises. Each of the three schools also has many sub-schools. The proliferation of such sub-schools is on account of the fact that all teachers, especially the popular ones, interpret Tai Chi slightly differently, and those differences are passed on. This is as it should be, however, because *Tai Chi is an art, not a science,* and therefore lends itself to artistic interpretation, though it is important for practitioners of adventurous temperament to distinguish between interpretation and bastardisation.

Chen style is the original, and involves slow and fast movements, sudden leaps and the explosive sound of 'cannon fist', wherein you smack the back of your wrist on to the other palm with a loud thwack and frighten all the birds away.

Yang, a student of Chen's, cheekily developed his own style, as did Wu, a student of both Chen and Yang.

The Wu style is the stranger/cheekier adaptation, some say aberration of the two, and involves sharper, less flowing, more angular, truncated movements than Chen or Yang.

Yang is by far the most popular (certainly with me), widely practised and probably the most sophisticated of the three. All movements are performed at even speed in an elegantly graceful yet powerful manner.

There is a short form, relatively recently devised in the early part of the twentieth century by Chen Man Ching, a sweet, inoffensive-looking little bloke, student of Yang, who could propel ten large men eight feet distance with a mere flick of the wrist and who, though purportedly enlightened, died of alcohol poisoning at seventy-five, with a smile on his face, apparently saying, 'Ha, ha, I've fooled you all!' (You hear many unbelievable stories of the lives and prowess of Tai Chi masters, and the amazing thing is they're all true. More or less.)

The short form, though, is mostly only used for teaching purposes as a bridge to learning the (proper) long form which they say has one hundred and eight movements, though personally I've never counted.

As well as the long form and its shorter derivative, there is the fast form, developed by Dung, employing jumps, horse kicks, and explosive cannon fist techniques, which is not only exciting to practise but also demonstrates clearly to self and others how Tai Chi Chuan is a potential killer, full-speed boxing style.

These are the empty hand (weaponless) forms, practice of which facilitates high conductivity of chi (energy) to the hands, elbow, shoulders, knees and feet for striking purposes. The addition of chi to your punch, chop, slap, elbow, barge, knee or kick, is equivalent to putting nuclear tips on your missiles, but without the hostile, overly metallic edge. After many years of practice, the chi permeates your bones, and though your movements are soft and flowing, to be struck by you feels like being thumped with a heavy iron bar wrapped in cotton-wool padding. It is not uncommon to see a full-grown opponent being effortlessly hurled eleven feet across the room by one little punch or slap. At higher levels you can even cause someone to drop on the spot from a distance of up to thirty-three feet, simply by firing off your chi at them with your mind.

To train for this, most practitioners get involved with weapons forms, as in sword, broadsword, staff, stick, dagger (and rubber biscuit). Of these, the rubber biscuit form is the least effective and is usually only practised by Taoist dogs. The principal aim with weapons forms is to be able to project your chi through an object, so when, say, that large stick hits your opponent on the head, it not only splits it in two, but he/she also gets a healing at the same time. This eventually leads to being able to direct your chi in a projectile stream with your mind and thus stop a man/woman at thirty-three feet, which is about as near to having your own remote pause control as you can get.

It's a strange paradox that a 'spiritual' system for attaining unwavering peace of mind and body, health and longevity, should have pugilism as its focus.

In fact, it is traditionally taught that if you actually have to resort to using your self-defensive skills in the physical, as opposed to psychic sense against another person, you've gone out of balance, overstepped your mark and have made a mistake.

Regular practice of Tai Chi stimulates/tonifies your defensive chi, and effectively builds up a psychic shielding mechanism which will protect you and keep you out of trouble. Moreover, your cheerful disposition and gentle good nature, both of which are cultivated as a by-product of practice, will endear you to one and all. Violent/aggressive tendencies are sublimated while martial skill is cultivated, making you far less prone to sudden fits of destructive rage.

It is important, though, that Tai Chi is practised with a 'combat-ready' focus, otherwise the movements look/feel namby pamby, ill-defined, point-less, limpid and weak, and you get nasty people bothering you and making veiled/unveiled threats to your slow-moving person when you practise in public places. This never occurs when you practise correctly, visualising your imaginary opponent so that your poses are true. Hostile passing imbeciles can feel your power, it seems, and are happy to leave you alone.

The form, whether empty-handed or beweaponed, always follows the same sequence of moves. This may sound samey, but the variation in poses is great enough to remain challenging for the rest of your life, at least.

No matter how negative, miserable, afraid, despairing, nervous, depressed, desperate or disparate you feel at the start of the form, you always feel better at the end, better enough at least to carry on being a hero for that day.

No matter how much your body feels like it's falling apart, if you're physically able to practise, it always feels joined up again by the practice end.

The long form contains all the information of Tai Chi and, if practised correctly, will theoretically train your chi to such a high level within, say, twenty years, that even without practising the two-person boxing/sparring exercises, or ever directly practising self-defence moves with a partner, you will still be invincible.

From personal experience, I'd say this is bullshit, as would many other practitioners, including Yang himself, were he here with me today, which is why great emphasis has always been placed on the two-person forms, or pushing hands as they are more commonly known.

Pushing hands

This is a 'boxing' meditation for two people, which trains you to be sensitive to someone else's energy, i.e. trains you to handle other people without losing your centre. It's like a formalised sparring match where your opponent's movement is automatically countered by one of yours. In this way, unless your opponent is a vicious bastard/bitch, or you are, practising pushing hands leaves you relatively injury free. Elementary push hands involves the use of one hand at a time only, and is conducted with your feet planted firmly on one spot. As you move through the more advanced stages, you use two hands in an at-first-sight complex series of manoeuvres known as 'grasping the sparrow's tail', and then stepping/footwork is introduced. This builds up to a two-person dance of great speed, requiring skill and precision, called ta lu, and eventually develops into the two-person form, otherwise known as the Dance of Equality which, if conducted at full speed and power, can be deadly if you don't pay attention.

As well as pushing hands, much training is devoted to learning, practising and drilling (repetitive action of punch-block, punch-block, etc.) the practical combative applications of all the various poses in the long form and weapons forms.

Once you've become literate in all that, you can proceed to free-form sparring, which is anyway what usually develops out of a good pushing-hands match, i.e. it often turns into a good old scrap.

I should point out at this stage that, though described as a boxing discipline, Tai Chi Chuan also develops and trains you to grapple with and throw your opponent great distances. Moreover, the poses are designed to train you to attack your opponent's vital points, which are the same points used in acupuncture/acupressure (shiatsu), and which, when attacked, can produce various responses from temporary paralysis of part or all of the body to outright death.

Unless you live to be eight hundred and three, it is fairly impossible to master/mistress [see *Impossibility of mastery*, p.116] all aspects of the training. Some practitioners emphasise the form, while others emphasise the two-person games and so on. But this just makes the training more enjoyable and enables you to engage in more useful exchanges of information with fellow practitioners.

Pushing hands, when it's good, is often better than sex. It is a most effective way of exponentially, synergistically multiplying your available energy levels and, on completion of a match, never fails to induce each of the parties involved to utter such sentiments as 'Wow, that was really great!'

Tai Chi propaganda summary

Tai Chi means supreme ultimate reality, meaning the highest/greatest/deepest you can go before you disappear altogether (into Wu Chi, that which lies beyond Tai Chi, i.e. absolute nothingness). In other words, practising the moves/playing your Tai Chi chops, takes you as high as you can go, experientially speaking and, in my humble opinion, provides a far more effective, long-lasting, reliable, good-for-health and ultimately relaxing trip than the strongest mind-altering drugs. And unlike any other drug, the more you do it the better it is for your health. In the long run, Tai Chi is much more effective for helping you overcome public shyness and developing true confidence than drugs like cocaine or alcohol and, moreover, provides an undeniably physical/experiential framework for you to grow spiritually [see *Cocaine as a social/personality stimulant* p.111 and *Alcohol as a social/personality lubricant* p.112]

Finally, for reasons no one has yet discovered but must have something to do with stimulation of melanin, people who practise Tai Chi every day outside, no matter the local climate, always have a healthy tan even in the dead of winter. And that's about all I can think of to say on the matter.

The stupendousness of Hsing I

Hsing I Chuan, as is its full name, means focused mind boxing. It is practised at a much faster speed than Tai Chi Chuan and is ostensibly more lethal to practise and impressive to observe.

As well as giving you flexibility, agility, health and superhuman levels of chi (energy) for use in self-defence and healing, regular practice develops an unassailable focus of mind or intent. Hsing I (pronounced shing yee) training teaches you to plough remorselessly right through your opponent using both your block/ward-off and your counter-strike as attacks. In this way, your defence simultaneously becomes your attack. By cultivating focused mind-intent during the practice, you learn to concentrate mental force in the centre of your forehead just above the line of your eyebrows (colloquial – third eye), which you then issue forth in an intense, high-velocity, laser-like projectile beam at and through your opponent's body to infinity beyond. Which is where your opponent is likely to find him/herself if you follow the beam with your physical person arranged precisely in the appropriate Hsing I boxing posture, until it meets your opponent's body with alarming speed and impact. In other words, the psycho-physical power acquirable/trainable through Hsing I is potentially devastating.

Far from breeding hoards of psychopathic human killing-machines, however, the practitioners of this stupendous art are, and have always been, renowned not only for their extraordinary powers and skills, but also for their conviviality, generosity and geniality. There must be something in the inherent blueprint of the system that reminds the practitioner to remain humble in the face of all that power, and to use it for the public good, like any true hero should, and not to wreak mindless havoc and destruction.

The training, like Tai Chi and Pa Kua, comprises eighty per cent solo work and twenty per cent partner work. The solo work consists of practising basic empty-hand (weaponless) forms, and weapons forms including long needle (like fat knitting needles) form, dagger form, stick form, short-sword form, broadsword form, short-staff form, long-staff form and spear form.

These are based on the Five Element and Twelve Animal forms, which together also comprise the Hsing I animal-element linking or long form. The Five Element (basic) forms consist of:

Metal, which corresponds to splitting/slicing actions
Water, which corresponds to drilling actions
Wood, which corresponds to crushing actions
Fire, which corresponds to pounding actions
Earth, which corresponds to crossing actions

These actions are practised as formalised, repetitive moves, while walking up and down in straight lines in similar fashion as when fencing, using the same rear-foot-dragging/stamping step, known in the business as 'follow step'.

While walking the lines, you concentrate on focusing your beam of intent and projecting it out through the centre of your forehead into infinity, or that sector of infinity that lies directly in your line of vision. Focusing on the beam remains a constant while your body-posture and local scenery change as you continue to walk the lines.

Of the five forms, metal/slicing is the most important because it

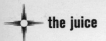

contains the basic Hsing I mechanism of lifting up and pulling down. This refers to the upwardly directed thrust of your arms as they 'lift' an oncoming strike out of the way by way of simultaneous defence and attack, and then proceed to 'pull down' on to the opponent's body/energy. Though hardly visible to the onlooker's naked eye, the effect of this lift-up-pull-down motion, is to first raise the opponent's chi, so he/she loses contact with his/her centre/'tan tien', becomes psycho-energetically scattered, and therefore allows him/herself to be physically scattered by your lifting action. At this point your lift turns into pull-down, whereby you descend with full force on to your opponent's body/energy and totally floor him/her.

After the Five Element forms come the Twelve Animal forms. These comprise the elements mixed with moves based on the way various animals have been observed to fight. When practising an animal form, you not only take on the (stylised) movement style of that animal, but also take on its spirit, which animates your movement.

This is especially useful in combative situations, as not only does it give you a vast pantheon of techniques and fighting styles to choose from, but also lends you the respective animal spirits to go with them. And as you know, in extreme situations where, as a hero, your self-defensive/combative skills may be called into service, every little bit of help you can get, you take.

Obviously, unless you spend an inordinate amount of time fighting people, the main benefits of these animal energies and spirits will show up in your daily working life to help you negotiate and duck'n'dive your way through the day.

The Twelve Animal forms consist of:

Dragon
Tiger
Monkey
Horse
Chicken
Turtle
Dove

Swallow
Snake
Falcon
Bear
Eagle

The Five Elements and Twelve Animals are then linked together in a certain set pattern to form the Hsing I long form.

As stupendous as the long form is to watch with its flying kicks, spins, sudden crouches and leaps, it's a thousand and eight times more stupendous to do. It's about the closest experience you can get to being a heat-seeking missile at full thrust.

The two-person training is similar to Tai Chi and involves a form of push hands which appears more like deadlock with both parties pushing on each other, neither seeming to move, until with a sudden explosion of energy, one of them, i.e. the one who lost it first, goes flying backwards.

There is also a series of short, set two-person forms and free-form sparring using full body-armour for the more daring practitioners, i.e. those with least to lose.

The experience of internal power generated by regular Hsing I is indeed so stupendous that if your system's not balanced enough, it can have profoundly disturbing effects. One master used to generate so much power in his lunchtime practice, he used to spend every afternoon in a coma. (Nutter.)

The profundity of Pa Kua

Pa Kua Chang, as is its full name, means 'eternally returning palm of the eight directions fighting method', and is sometimes also known as Divine Boxing (gods in a punch-up).

It's based on the I Ching [see *Making decisions – pendulums, Tarot, I Ching* p.61] and, like the eight (cosmic) directions or trigram symbols (Pa Kua) of the I Ching, makes use of eight different palm-striking positions. These correspond to the Strong, Yielding, Inciting, Dangerous, Resting, Penetrating, Light-giving and Joyful.

The form is practised walking in tight circles, with the arms in various positions based on the movements of the snake, lion, dragon and hawk and is not dissimilar in appearance to the dance of the Whirling Dervishes. It feels like spinning round in circles as a child, but without the dizziness. To the contrary, your mind feels sharp as a razor and your vision is entirely focused. While walking the idea is not to resist the strong altered-(trance)-state that Pa Kua (pronounced ba guah) induces, but to go into it deeply while remaining fully focused, centred and alert. In the Pa Kua trance you are elevated above the constricted view of the linear progression of time and can see into the future or past at will. In this way it is the same as the I Ching oracle.

Practising the form, you walk the circle in a counter-clockwise direction, for as many revolutions as you like with your arms held in a certain, fixed on-guard position, and when ready, perform the first direction change. This consists of a series of self-defensive postures linked together in a similar way as in Tai Chi, which turns you round so you're walking in the other (clockwise) direction.

When you've had enough, you repeat the first direction change in mirror image and find yourself walking counter-clockwise again. You go through this procedure seven more times in each direction, making eight counter-clockwise circuits alternating with eight clockwise circuits. Each time you make a direction change, however, the series of moves involved changes, according to set sequential patterns, until by the time you finally arrive at the end, after anything from ten minutes to an hour later, you've gone through all the fighting techniques in the system, including chops, finger jabs, slaps, blows, rippings, throws, grabs, kicks, kneeings and floorings.

The basic empty-palm form can also be performed holding two short scythes or long daggers, which is when you look (and feel) like a human rotor-blade killing machine. In fact one famous master was said to have killed off twenty troops who had come to arrest him on some trumped up charge, in this very manner, before finally being killed. Do not attempt this at home.

When walking the circle counter-clockwise, you are stepping out of your past, and thereby releasing yourself from the grip of the consequences of your former actions, i.e. your karma (yes, it's that powerful).

When walking the circle in a clockwise direction, you're stepping into the future, i.e. your new good, which now shows up in whichever way you choose at the time, appropriate, satisfying, exhilarating, scintillating, wealthy, and/or famous, for example. Pa Kua practise cleans your karmic slate for you, gives you enormous psychic power, prevents and possibly cures lymphatic cancer, generally makes your energy go round with an undeniable whoosh, gives you a palm that you can knock a water buffalo out with, makes your body look fit and lean, and gives you the ability to be always at the back of and therefore in control of your opponent.

The combative aspects of Pa Kua are trained in a relatively straight-forward way, considering it's all done walking round and round in circles. Like Tai Chi and Hsing I, there are a number of pushing-hands-style exercises, applications of the postures drilled, and free-form sparring undertaken, often with the benefit of body-armour. Pa Kua masters/mistresses are famous for stunts like jumping ten feet in the air from standing, walking up walls and along ceilings, if you believe that kind of thing, but as well as such exotic benefits, Pa Kua practice also offers you the opportunity to proudly say, 'Yes!', the next time someone accuses you of going round and round in circles (you nutter).

'Nuff propaganda?

EXCELLENCE NUMBER THREE: HEALING (WATER ELEMENT)

Taoist healing methods include acupuncture, acupressure, and moxibus-tion (burning mugwort herb) applied to vital points, herbs, massage, joint manipulation and energy healing. Of these, energy healing is the most powerful. Various combinations of the other methods are traditionally only used to prepare someone for an energy healing. It is also the easiest to learn initially and needs no form training. In fact, the less formal train-ing you have, the better. As with any art form, real training only comes from experience and it takes anything up to an entire lifetime to start getting anywhere near a serious handle on it.

Why would you want to heal people?

To help relieve their suffering.

Why?

Because you're a hero. (End of story.)

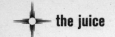 **the juice**

Any other motivation, seeking kudos, glory, fame, wealth (income), goodwill-credit, escape from working in an office, etc. is a slipstream/ secondary motivation, even if you don't realise it yet.

When you want to heal people, it's because love is pushing to come through you. If you practise meditation [see *Meditation* p.126] and/or martial arts [see *Martial arts* p.138] for some months, i.e. long enough to feel some tangible benefit, the spontaneous self-healing that occurs of itself as a natural by-product of the practice, impels you to want to share the joy/excitement/pleasure you derive from that with others in any way you can.

The most natural way of sharing that joy, i.e. love, is to place your hands on someone (willing) with intent to transmit your love and, without doing anything else to interfere, simply allow your hands to be the conduits which conduct that love into the core energy field of said willing someone's person, i.e. heal them.

What will that do?

It's like plugging someone into the universal source of all energy.

But don't you have to be extremely tuned in, centred and holy enlightened to plug someone into the universal source of all energy?

Not really.

But if you're just a regular prat, doing the odd bit of meditation here and there, doing a bit of Tai Chi now and then, running around trying to be rich and famous with your head full of you (and money and sex), how can you be a conduit for universal healing energy?

When you put your hands on someone with intent to transmit love (spiritual), it turns on a switch which opens the flow of universal healing energy (UHE) and as that flow kicks in, it overrides your local self, like a car on a flyover passing over the traffic on the busy city streets beneath it. You could be simultaneously engaged in idle gossip/chit-chat, and the UHE would still be transmitted.

Wouldn't the healing be more powerful, though, if you concentrated on what you were doing?

Of course.

Would meditation and martial arts help you concentrate your healing powers?

Meditate while you heal someone. It will help you still your mind and focus the UHE as it comes through. Doing a martial arts training session before healing someone strengthens your body and psyche so that you're more energetically protected and less likely to pick up that someone's negativity/ill energy/germs. Training also opens your internal energy channels and thus intensifies the flow of UHE through you as a vessel/conduit.

Where does that UHE enter your body when you're healing someone? Through the back of your neck.

What effect will it have on someone when you pump UHE into his or her body?

UHE will enter that person's internal energy field through whichever physical access point you've chosen and circulate, acting as a catalyst activating and mobilising that person's own inherent healing energy and intelligence. That intelligence will know exactly what the body needs to do with the healing energy.

But what if there's nothing actually wrong with someone and you just feel like putting your hands on them with intent to transmit UHE?

It always helps to activate and stimulate someone's inherent self-healing energy. It boosts the immune response and helps prevent disease.

But what if someone's got a broken leg, can you help that get better faster?

Yes. Place your hand on the break, through the plaster cast if necessary.

How often would you need to do it?

As often as you felt the inner prompting to do so. It's the/your spirit which guides you in these matters.

Wouldn't it be hard to get through plaster cast?

A bit. But UHE is stronger than that. You don't have to be touching the body for it to be transmitted effectively. In fact, often the transmission is much more powerful when the hands are held one, two and even three feet away from the body surface.

Is that how absent healing works?

Yes. Absent healing is the most powerful form of UHE transmission because it works through the power of pure thought and doesn't have to pass through the resistance of physical bodies.

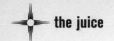

What if someone has a serious, life-threatening disease, can you he
them get better?

Maybe.

Is there any point trying?

Of course. Miracles happen when you transmit UHE successfully.

Could you stop someone dying like that?

Maybe.

You don't seem too sure.

There are too many variables to consider to be able to give a clear y
or no to such a hypothetical question. Perhaps that person has ha
enough here and the time has come for them to die. In that case, tl
healing you give them will help them die more peacefully. If, on the oth
hand, they still have more time, your healing may give them the jum
start they need to get back on the road. Then of course it also depends
how clearly you're transmitting that day.

How long does a healing take?

About two fractions of a nano-second.

As quick as that?

It doesn't occur in time. It occurs out of time in the eternal momen
But to set things up for that to occur usually takes about ten minut
feeding-in time and about the same on the way out.

Now what the doodle do you mean by that?

For that moment to occur usually requires you to keep your hands
or above someone's body for about ten minutes before the UHE star
pumping. It could be quicker, but that's a hypothetical average. After tl
UHE has done its job of catalysing that person's own self-healing energ
intelligence, that is, once the healing's been done, it usually takes abo
ten minutes to withdraw gracefully. It's like making love. If a good co
nection's just been made, you don't want to pull out too fast.

Is it wrong for you to charge money for healing people?

Yes. But it's perfectly fair, reasonable and correct to charge for yo
time. (As long as you don't take the piss.)

How do you start healing people?

By starting to heal people. Start with your family and close frienc
Ask, 'Would you like a healing?' If one says yes and you do it and th

158

ke it, everyone will want you to heal them. Don't start charging for your me until you've had enough experience healing people to feel confident nough to be yourself while engaged in the actual transmission process nd don't feel the need to prove anything. If you start charging too soon will cause you anxiety, which is counter-productive in the long run.

How much pressure do you apply when you place your hands on?

Four ounces.

Why four ounces?

Three is too little to establish intelligent contact. Five is too intrusive nd manipulative.

Is that intended to be a precise measurement of the weight you apply uring transmission?

It's another way of saying – do it with love.

Can you harm someone by healing them?

Only if you stick your fingers in someone's eye or that kind of thing.

Will someone feel better straight away after you heal them?

Yes.

But will their symptoms clear up immediately?

Probably not. It usually takes between twenty-four and forty-eight ours for that person's inherent self-healing energy-intelligence to com-lete its task and for an improvement to become noticeable.

Can someone have an unpleasant reaction to a transmission?

Yes. If there is a big toxic build-up, those toxins will be stirred up by he healing causing the symptoms to grow worse initially before improv-ng.

If you want to increase the effectiveness of your healing, are there spe-ific physical access points through which to enter someone's inner nergy field which will be more effective than others?

Yes.

Where are they?

ealing holds

he following is a general healing sequence which can be used safely to reat effect as a tonic for anyone at any time in any mental and/or physi-al condition (except dead).

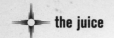 **the juice**

Obviously, when there is a specific pain, put your hand there before embarking on this sequence.

This sequence is designed to promote balance of yin and yang ch (energy), by clearing the head and chest, opening the breathing passages settling the belly and drawing energy towards the 'tan tien' (two thumb widths down and in from the navel), and thence into the kidneys to b recharge and recirculated.

If transmission is successful, the projected effects will be a noticeabl reduction of stress factor and increase of relaxation, self-peace, self-love self-acceptance, self-confidence and clarity of mind. Immune respons will be increased. Stress-related conditions such as mania, high blood pressure, insomnia, panic attacks, headaches, chest pains, breathlessnes and indigestion will be eased. In addition, it will help regulate bowe movements, menstrual flow and appetite.

Depending on the state of patient's health and how on form you are a the time, it can take up to seven sessions over a twenty-two-day period t ensure a radical shift in patient's inner-energy field, leading to genuin reversal/amelioration of symptoms. Expect to see changes, subtle anc otherwise, within three days of the second session, but do not attacl yourself to results. Merely immerse yourself in the healing itself and le the UHE (universal healing energy) do the rest.

Though it is perfectly permissible to perform only one or more of th following holds, it is advised to follow the suggested sequence for th least unpredictable, most stable and satisfying outcome.

Start-up head hold

Patient sitting or lying.

You, standing or sitting behind (them).

State your intention (to yourself) to relieve patient of suffering and t increase health/comfort/peace/longevity levels.

Check your own posture. Check self-comfort levels. Check self-relaxatior levels. Adjust accordingly.

Check your breathing. Slow down and regulate the tempo.

Place your palms one on each side of patient's head.

Wait.

Do nothing.

Relax.

Visualise the star-symbol [see Hardcore *technique: Placing the star-symbol p.136]. With your mind, place one star-symbol in the centre of each of your palms and one in the centre of patient's brain.*

Visualise a stream of UHE (universal healing energy) lit up in white-golden light, entering your body through the back of your neck, in the centre, where your neck meets your skull.

Visualise/feel/imagine-you-feel that UHE streaming through your two shoulders and down through the inside of your arms, into your hands, out through the centre of your palms (star-symbols), in through the sides of the patient's head and into the heart of their star-symbol.

Wait until you instinctively feel the transmission is complete. (There are no guidelines for this.)

Remove your hands extremely slowly, like you're reeling silk from a cocoon, by taking them out to the sides until each is two feet distant from side of patient's head. Shake your hands as if shaking off brackish water to release any negative chi you may have picked up inadvertently.

This hold balances left and right sides of patient's inner-energy field/brain/body, and clears the mind.

Front/back head hold

Patient sitting.

You, sitting at patient's left side.

Place your right palm over the back of patient's skull (with four ounces) so that it neatly cups the occipital (rear skull) bone from left to right.

Place your left palm over patient's forehead so that it neatly cups the frontal bone from left to right.

Wait.

Do nothing.

Relax.

As before, visualise the star-symbol [see Hardcore Technique: Placing the star-symbol *p.136]. With your mind, place one star-symbol in the centre of each of your palms, one in the centre of patient's brain, and one in the patient's 'tan tien' region, two thumb-widths down and in from the navel.*

Visualise a stream of UHE (universal healing energy) lit up in flashlight-blue-golden light, entering your body through the back of your neck, in the centre, where your neck meets your skull.

Visualise/feel/imagine-you-feel that UHE streaming through your right shoulder and down through the inside of your right arm, into your hand, out through the centre of your palm (star-symbol), in through the back of patient's head through their star-symbol, on through their forehead and into your left palm, whence it bounces back down through the front of patient's body into the star-symbol in their 'tan tien'.

In other words, feel/visualise the stream of UHE running from back to front of the patient's head, then running downwards to the lower abdomen.

Wait until you instinctively feel the transmission is complete, i.e. you imagine their belly is full.

Remove your hands extremely slowly, like you're reeling silk from a cocoon, by taking them out to the front and back until each is two feet distant from patient's head. Shake your hands as if shaking off brackish water to release any negative chi you may have picked up inadvertently.

This hold removes excess mental energy (heat) from the head and upper parts and sends it down to the kidneys to strengthen the entire system.

Chest and upper-back hold

Patient sitting.

You, sitting at patient's left side.

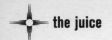

Place your right palm over patient's upper back (with four ounces) so that it cups the area between the shoulder-blades from left to right.

Place your left palm over patient's chest at the level of the nipples so that it lies across the chest comfortably from left to right.

Wait.

Do nothing.

Relax.

Visualise the star-symbol [see Hardcore techniques: Placing the star-symbol *p.136]. With your mind, place one star-symbol in the centre of each of your palms, one in the centre of patient's chest, and one in the patient's 'tan tien' region, two thumb-widths down and in from the navel.*

Visualise a stream of UHE (universal healing energy) lit up in rose-golden light, entering your body through the back of your neck, in the centre, where your neck meets your skull.

Visualise/feel/imagine-you-feel that UHE streaming through your right shoulder and down through the inside of your right arm, into your hand, out through the centre of your palm (star-symbol), in through the patient's back through their star-symbol, on through their chest and into your left palm, whence it bounces back down through the front of patient's body into the star-symbol in their 'tan tier.'.

In other words, feel/visualise the stream of UHE running from back to front of patient's upper body then running downwards to the lower abdomen.

Wait until you instinctively feel the transmission is complete, i.e. you imagine their belly is full/hot.

Remove your hands extremely slowly, like you're reeling silk from a cocoon, by taking them out to the front and back until each is two feet distant from patient's upper body. Shake your hands as if shaking off brackish water to release any negative chi you may have picked up inadvertently.

This hold relieves energetic/physical congestion in the chest, collects all excess heat from the heart and lungs and puts it back in the kidneys (boiler room) where it belongs.

Upper-belly hold

Patient lying on back.

You, sitting at patient's right side facing towards his/her head.

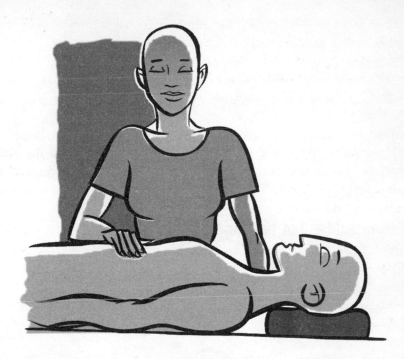

Place your right palm across patient's upper abdomen from right to left so that it neatly cups the solar plexus region in the soft triangle formed on two sides by the lower ribs.

Wait.

Do nothing.

Relax.

Visualise the star-symbol [see Hardcore *techniques: Placing the star-symbol p.136]. With your mind, place one star-symbol in the centre of your right palm, and one in the centre of patient's upper abdomen.*

Visualise a stream of UHE (universal healing energy) lit up in green-golden light, entering your body through the back of your neck, in the centre, where your neck meets your skull.

Visualise/feel/imagine-you-feel that UHE streaming through your right shoulder and down through the inside of your right arm, into your hand, out through the centre of your palm (star-symbol), in through the patient's upper belly through their star-symbol, and see it radiate outwards until the entire upper abdominal area is suffused with it.

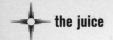

Wait until you instinctively feel the transmission is complete, i.e. you imagine their upperbelly is completely and deeply relaxed.

Remove your hand extremely slowly, like you're reeling silk from a cocoon, by lifting it vertically off patient's body to a height of two feet. Shake your hands as if shaking off brackish water to release any negative chi you may have picked up inadvertently.

This hold unblocks and regulates breathing (diaphragm) mechanism, which is essential to any/every healing, and unblocks stagnant emotional energy (resentment, anxiety, angst, anguish, grief, melancholia, or any combination of these).

Closing hold – 'tan tien' and kidney hold

Patient sitting.

You, sitting at patient's left side.

Place your right palm over patient's lower back (with four ounces) so that it cups the area between the lower ribs and the hip bones from left to right.

Place your left palm over patient's lower abdomen just below the level of the

navel so that it neatly cups the belly comfortably from left to right.

Wait.

Do nothing.

Relax.

Visualise the star-symbol [see Hardcore technique: Placing the star-symbol p.136]. With your mind, place one star-symbol in the centre of each of your palms, one in the patient's 'tan tien' region, two thumb-widths down and in from the navel, and one in the perineum, between the legs, directly in front of the anus and behind the genitals.

Visualise a stream of UHE (universal healing energy) lit up in yellow-golden light, entering your body through the back of your neck, in the centre, where your neck meets your skull.

Visualise/feel/imagine-you-feel that UHE streaming through your right shoulder and down through the inside of your right arm, into your hand, out through the centre of your palm (star-symbol), in through the patient's lower back through their kidneys, through the star-symbol in their 'tan tien' and into your left palm, whence it bounces back down through the front of patient's belly into the star-symbol between their legs.

In other words, feel/visualise the stream of UHE running from back to front of patient's lower body then running downwards to the perineum.

Wait until you instinctively feel the transmission is complete, i.e. you imagine his/her belly and perineum is full/hot.

Remove your hands extremely slowly, like you're reeling silk from a cocoon, by taking them out to the front and back until each is two feet distant from patient's lower body. Shake your hands as if shaking off brackish water to release any negative chi you may have picked up inadvertently.

This hold relieves energetic/physical congestion in the kidneys, intestines, bladder, reproductive system and sexual organs, strengthens immune response, and generally grounds/earths/roots patient in material reality, ready to continue with his/her life.

Hands-off healing

Perform the above holds individually or in sequence with your hands held at an average distance of fourteen inches from patient's body. Employ exactly the same UHE visualisation and star-symbol placements as when doing hands-on.

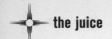

Pay extra attention to relaxing your shoulders and arms.

Hands-off is more profound than hands-on, as it works on the finer, less dense layers of chi (energy) in the outer-energy field (aura). This in turn affects the inner-energy field, which over the course of the following days, weeks and even months, produces sizeable shifts in physical and mental health.

Hands-on is more effective for instigating immediate change in the short-term, such as pain relief/removal (physical and emotional/ mental). Hands-off is more effective for instigating/perpetuating long-term change (for the better).

For best all-round healing results, employ a combination of both. Start with hands-on in each hold, then progress to hands-off before moving on to the next hold.

Self-healing

Use all the above holds, as well as any you discover on your own, hands-on and hands-off, on yourself as well.

It is perfectly feasible and advisable to treat yourself to at least one weekly session of self-healing in this manner.

Not only will this help you keep in psychic/emotional/physical health, but the inner experience engendered is the best way to educate yourself to heal others. You can only be truly effective at healing others if you're effective at healing yourself. This is the true meaning of 'healer, heal thyself'.

Absent healing

This is for when you want to heal someone, whether unbidden or by invitation, with whom you are not sharing the immediate vicinity, and are not likely to be imminently doing so.

It makes no difference how much physical distance or how obstructed the terrain is between you. UHE (universal healing energy) is not in any way bounded by limitations of time and space.

To perform an absent healing, simply perform the above healing holds, individually or in sequence, without the use of your hands, i.e. just by visualising it. Make use of star-symbol placement.

Pay special focus to any particular area or aspect you know needs attention. If, for example, you're sending absent healing to someone who's undergoing a liver transplant, spend time visualising green-gold light surrounding and infusing his/her new liver and making it feel at home in its new host-body. Place the star-symbol there. To close the healing, visualise patient in glowing state of health with problem fixed.

Healing while negotiating and mediating

By healing lots of people, the way you look at people starts to change. You start to see people as souls needing healing rather than objects of hate, resentment, derision or fear.

Healing people gets you used to seeing through the surface illusion/mask/outer appearance/personality (we've all got one) to the pure soul within.

This starts happening spontaneously and automatically after a while, so that if/when you find yourself confronted by hostility or adverse energy coming towards your person from another, you are able instantaneously to see past that to the soul inside, which is unconsciously asking for love. Note that, however, because this love-request is unconscious, it probably won't work to break cover, i.e. blow the charade [see *Living theatre* p.40] and come out with something soppy like, 'I love you!', especially in a business meeting/police interview/bank, etc.

Instead, choose to give them a surreptitious (distant) hands-off healing, complete with star-symbol placement [see *Hardcore techniques: Placing the star-symbol* p.136]. Do not be invasive about it. Simply allow the process to occur on its own, while outwardly you carry on as normal/abnormal. In the moments that follow, it is not unlikely that you'll witness an obvious change for the better in your antagonist's energy/demeanour/disposition/behaviour towards you, without a word about it being said. (That's magic.)

This is especially efficacious for use at business meetings or mediation sessions involving any form of negotiation of what's fair for all parties concerned. Healing equates to balancing, equates to making fair.

Healing is a continuous process. It's simply a matter of tapping in to that stratum of reality where the healing's going on. Aspire to maintain an unbroken connection to that and before long, people will be healed

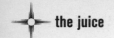

simply by being in your presence, or even just by thinking of you. When you're moving at this level, it's very hard for others to take advantage of you by attempting to place you in an unfair position, because the reflection being mirrored by your person (back to them) is too strong. It would have been like trying to rip off Mother Teresa. You just wouldn't do it. And if you're dealing with someone who would, don't.

EXCELLENCE NUMBER FOUR: COMPOSITIONAL SKILLS (WOOD ELEMENT)

This is, traditionally, music and poetry composition. Composition, itself a composite word, comes from the Latin meaning 'positioning things together/well arranged'.

Thus positioned, the hitherto disparate parts of the composite form a new entity with a life/identity of its own, far greater than the sum of its components. (That's synergy.)

What are you talking about?

You're walking along, in Amsterdam, say, and you hear the snatch of a tune in your head. That's nice, you think to yourself. Eleven or twelve minutes later, you hear it again, this time with a few more bars tacked on the end. Very nice, you think, and begin to search your mind for all available current chart, back catalogue and archive information to ascertain whether this tune is 'originating' with you or if it's already been done.

After extensive scanning, lasting about forty seconds in real time, your search shows up nothing, maybe a vague resemblance to the final movement in Sibelius's sixth symphony, but yours has got a harder edge and anyway he's dead, so you don't have to worry about copyright.

A little later at dinner, the tune comes back, this time going right up to the bridge and into the chorus. The middle eight comes as you drop a sugar lump in your coffee, wondering if it's a good idea as you need to sleep, and just as you get to 'what the hell!' the harmonies kick in. As you perform finger-and-thumb-wiggle-in-space-to-ask-for-bill procedures, you notice you're doing it in time to a beat, and by the time you stand up, you've got a new tune.

What's *that* got to do with synergy?

Everything. The component parts of the tune come together through your own self-organisational skills [see *Organisational skills* p.175] to form a tune, whose value as an information-carrier is far greater than the infor-mation-carrying value of any of the individual component parts.

Information?

Yes. You orgainise bits of information into a particular configuration in your mind, which can then be translated, through the use of various actions and tools, into a manifest entity (product), for others to enjoy (buy/exchange for). That's composition. And it doesn't apply only to music (of course).

The organisation of information into a new and original configuration, i.e. the act of composing, applies to all creative modalities. Visual, sonic, literary, graphic, photographic, performance, filmic, informational, func-tional and dramatic art, all require composing, that is, organising into a presentable/marketable shape before they can be enjoyed by others in any sizeable or significant way.

To assist you in your organising/composing activities, make liberal use of external memory support facilities, such as writing/drawing it down on paper/screen, or recording into a personal recording gadget as soon as possible after initial receipt of all information-fragments/units.

Channelling skills

For the sake of experiment, assume all information-fragments arriving on your internal doorstep, from sources other than others, is coming from consciousness of a higher-than-human realm [see *Discoveries and following your Muse* p.172].

This is the realm of your own higher self.

It's also the realm of the higher selves of Krishna, Bach, Lao Tsu, John Lennon, Jesus, Andy Warhol, Marilyn Monroe and Fred Nietzsche, to name but a very few.

You never know who's sending you messages from there. Could just be your own self, or it could be anyone or combination of anyones from

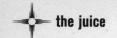

anywhere at any time in the entire universe, from your old Aunt Annie to Zombor, King/Queen of Zednov 3. You just never know. So you have to train yourself to be alert to any incoming information. When intensely otherwise occupied you can check in later when you have a quiet moment, just like e-mail.

To do this, sit quietly until inwardly and outwardly settled.

Focus your intent on connecting to the relevant higher-realms network and once connected, i.e. receptive, shout out, 'Have you got any messages for me?'

Then wait in the meditative/mentally empty state, and if there's something there for you, grab the bugger and start composing [see Developing receptivity p.94].

This describes the act of channelling. The composition part is where you take that pure information you've just channelled and run it past your own personal set of reality-filters which, depending on how clear/opaque/coloured/distorted they are, determine the nature, quality and style of the product which may finally materialise. Both channelling and composition skills improve with practice.

The major block to channelling is a busy mind, which is why daily meditation (and martial arts) practice is strongly recommended in this respect.

The major block to composing is your internalised critic telling you it's crap all the time [see *Shoot the critic* p.28].

Sometimes it seems to take great courage to commit to composing something in whatever kind of art form you're engaged in the pursuit of, but it doesn't. All you have to do is start, and if you don't like what you come up with, bin it.

Discovering and following your Muse

In Greek mythology, there are nine goddesses/Muses presiding over the various arts (hence music and museum, as art-storehouse).

Legend has it that any parcel of original information you derive/channel from higher realms for the purposes of composition (transformation/reshuffling into a product), is inspired, i.e. given unto you by one of these nine goddesses or Muses.

With the advent of neo-classicism and later, romanticism, various poets and the like took up the notion of each artist 'having' his/her own personal Muse. And why not? So, if you find yourself with neo-classical or romantic inclinations one day, don't be ashamed, to the contrary, milk it for all it's worth.

Like any other goddesses/gods, Muses may only exist as thoughtforms of your own. On the other hand they may not. They may actually be real autonomous entities (RAEs), susceptible to your supplications. Either way, if you think/believe/imagine them to be RAEs, i.e. if you imbue the thoughtform with power, then RAEs they'll be.

To make contact with your Muse, proceed as normal with your accustomed mode of opening lines, i.e. 'Hello/Yo/All right, Muse!', etc. Then wait for a response. Style of Muse-response varies according to degree of inner-theatricality levels of supplicator, but is usually experienced as a vague sense of the presence of 'Other', accompanied by a subtle altering of the tone of your mental state. Some Muse-supplicators report a quickening of the pulse and an excited sensation in the chest.

Now ask 'You got anything for me today?'

At this point, the dialogue either takes off on its own or it doesn't. You can't force it. Especially with a goddess. I mean, what do they need *you* for!

Because my personal set of filters is uniquely distorted into just the shape she's looking for at the moment to get her new idea made into a Hollywood movie, and no one else could do the job?

Don't kid yourself. She's putting it out with an open invitation to everyone to make a pitch for it. If you don't do it, someone else will.

Exactly the same?

Maybe. Doesn't matter, it'll be enough the same for her.

But what I compose might change the course of human culture for ever. If someone else composed it, the culture might go along totally different lines. Wouldn't that be a shame for me, for her?

Maybe.

Is there a way to win the loyalty of my Muse?

Yes. Be loyal to her.

How do I do that?

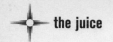

Simply by letting go and relaxing. Let whatever wants to com
through you come through freely, without you getting in the way, wit
your ideas, opinions and judgements. If it's a book, write, just let it com
Stop thinking so much. Same with a painting, a piece of music or wha
ever. Let it come through however it wants to and sort it out later [se
Importance of editing p.197].

Take a vow to yourself and/or to your Muse to be always availabl
(within twenty-four hours) to do channelling and composition job
whenever they come up, and then stick to that. That's how you win he
loyalty. Otherwise she'll treat you as a mere dilettante and won't bothe
with you again till you mend your ways [see *Persistence of the hero* p.33]

On being a cultural terrorist

With everything having been done that could shock people (in a cultura
sense), and people being no longer shockable, there is little gain i
attempting to shock people overtly to gain their attention (and thus bu
your product). People (mostly) are too sophisticated for that.

This does not mean that the spirit of cultural terrorism is dead, or eve
gone underground. Quite the reverse, in fact. The whole thing (huma
society) has become one big cultural terror. Beneath the surface, perhap
a few more layers deeper down in some more than in others, people ar
shitting themselves!

Offering succour, i.e. inner peace, is more likely to attract public atten
tion, slowly but surely, than offering more shocks. People inur
themselves to shock. It's inevitable and necessary for daily surviva
which itself provides a form of self-administered aversion therapy. I
other words, people consider themselves unsophisticated, i.e. easy to
take advantage of and therefore vulnerable, if they show themselve
(even to themselves) to be shocked by anything (cultural). Tits on pag
three, presidential knobs, rampant cocaine addiction in the world of high
finance, bloody human half-heads lying near their former (massacred
bodies – people are inured.

Modern cultural terrorism entails fusing hitherto disparate cultural/cre
ative strands into a new/original combination/configuration, and the
planting the results like a bomb in a shopping mall. The thematic messag

f (post-) modern culture is nothing lasts. Everything's changing faster and ster as the spread of information via digital/electronic/satellite systems celerates.

This is not, then, necessarily the time/epoch to be stuck on producing masterpiece. If you've got one coming through, fine. But if you're olding up your creative flow until you're ready to do one, don't. This is the time of smash'n'grab, cut'n'paste, mix'n'match. This is *not* the time or being precious with your creativity.

Channel stuff through, organise it and get it out as fast as you can. hannel, compose, disseminate. And don't hang about.

This is not to say you should be bringing out shoddy crap just because he world's probably spinning out of control and you want to get your oyalty payments in before it does so you can buy a patch of land on some istant planet and start again. Just that you shouldn't slow yourself/your reative output down because you're so busy searching for the perfect orm of expression that you're missing the gems that are trying to come hrough you now.

Have a pop.

Don't listen to anyone who tells you it can't be done. If you can't get a lm crew, do it yourself on a palmcorder. And if they tell you you can't roadcast that kind of quality, don't listen. If your film is good enough 'll get broadcast even if it's shot on a rubber band (if you know how to o that). And if it's not, the next one will be, and if not that, the next.

That way you'll either get one on eventually or you'll die. Which isn't he same as saying if you don't get your film on, you'll die (except even- ually).

The important thing is to keep those projects coming, and sooner or ater ...

rganisational skills

nce you've composed, i.e. organised incoming information into a product, ou have to organise reality to accommodate the induction of that composi- on into material form. This requires you map out a scheme and a timetable.

Just as with designing the masterplan for your life [see *Creating a mas- rplan vs. surrendering to destiny* p.90], most schemes are best laid out in

175

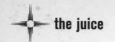

diagram form rather than in list form, enabling you laterally to scan an notice all the different strands and their links together at a sweep of th eye.

Once you know what your task-load consists of, you can prioritise, i.e make a list of tasks in projected optimum chronological order.

Once you know what has to be done when, you can estimate how lon each task will take (always overestimate this).

Then you can prepare a projected timetable. Do not indulge in self deception at this point. Be realistic. Consult your diary and be sure that al other commitments will also be served by the timetable you are preparing

Then all you have to do is follow it. It's like painting by numbers.

Following this process is, obviously, even more important whe working with others on a project, and it is vital that all parts of the plan priorities and timetable scheme are discussed and agreed upon fully b all involved parties both before and during the proposed timeframe o the project.

However, before you can organise the elements of a project into cohesive plan, you have to know what those elements are. And for tha you need to heed the following:

Brainstorming

This applies to working on a project solo or with a partner/collabora tor/group, no matter the nature of that project, creative or otherwise.

Say you're writing a book like this one with a group of collaborators. On person, you, perhaps, stands by the white shiny board on an easel and wait with fat felt-tip at the ready. Everyone involved now starts calling out item they think should be included in the book. You judge nothing. Simply writ what they call out on the board, cancelling duplications as they arise Encourage everyone to go into uninhibited freeflow. Just keep writing it on the board, no matter how stupid or irrelevant it seems. Eventually the stean runs out and after the last straggling suggestions come home, you replace th cap on the marker pen and sit down with the others to debate the relativ importance and relevance of each item suggested.

Only then can you set about organising all those various strands into comprehensible/comprehesive order.

When working on a solo project, always have a full-on brainstorming session with yourself, imagining all the different internalised people within you calling out their various suggestions, and just keep writing them down. (You don't need a presentation board for this. A4 paper will suffice for solo work.)

Don't judge or censor the suggestions coming through. Just keep them coming. Only after one or more of such self-brainstorming sessions when you feel comfortable that you've got all possible elements of the project down, can you then proceed to the organising stage.

This channel-brainstorm-organise approach to projects also applies to writing business letters/e-mails/faxes, press releases, advertisements and business plans, all of which should be accorded the same care and creative focus as the project itself, especially the press release!

Becoming mediagenic (creating a multimedia context for your message to the world)

Being mediagenic means coming through with a message/product that will translate easily into at least two or more media.

It's like being photogenic or telegenic. You/your product have to look good carried in as many media as possible, because with the currently huge proliferation of media channels available, and currently declining human birthrate, it means that there's a dwindling number of punters to be shared out amongst a growing number of information/entertainment-disseminating channels. And though this encourages specialisation, thus enabling advertisers, upon whom the channels depend for their income, to target their audiences more accurately, it also means there's less audience for each channel.

Hence the more channels you can have a presence in, the more people are going to hear your message (obviously).

If your message, therefore, is packaged in such a way that it can be carried efficiently on TV, film, radio, Internet, CD Rom, Audio CD, DVD, *and* in live performance, not only are you laughing, but your reach will be extended exponentially.

In reality, it is often only practical to achieve this through collaboration

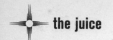

with other artists whose style, philosophy, cultural colours and message temporarily dovetails with your own.

Mediagenicism also depends on the way you organise or package the information contained in your message/product. The more art forms you can express your message through the better.

The different art forms are:

Visual Arts, including painting, photography, grafitti, graphic design, advertising posters, etc.
Sonic Arts, i.e. music.
Visual-Sonic Combination Art, including TV commercials/ programmes, movies, etc.
Literary Art, including poetry/lyrics, prose (non-fiction and fiction) and journalism.
Performance Art, including dance, theatre, concerts, circus, opera, etc.
Functional/Tactile Art, including architecture, sculpture/3D, furni- ture, Aston Martins, interior design, fashion (clothing/shoes/ accessories, etc.).
Interactive Multimedia Installation/Performance Art, i.e. setting up an installation where people can experience your message in words (written/spoken/sung), images (still and moving) on monitors and projected on screens, music (live and recorded), live performance (acting, playing music, miming, dancing, conjuring, hypnotising, per- forming martial arts, juggling, tumbling, flying-trapeze, clowning, live-sex, etc.), 3D objects (furniture, equipment, buttons to press, walkways to cross, ladders to climb, poles to slide down, chairs to sit in, beds to lie on, etc.), enhanced by lighting programmes and even smells. This can be on any scale, from bedroom size to stadium.

So there are the outlets/media and there are the art forms you can put through them. The f'n'f game is about picking as many of each as you can through which to express your message and putting them together in as many combinations as possible without spreading yourself too thin at any one time [see *Doing one thing at a time in rapid succession* p.115].

However, if you're stuck for an art form and you just can't decide which if any are appropriate for you to express yourself through, try writing.

The written word

The written word has great power as an entertainment/information carrying facility and is also great fun, i.e. highly entertaining to play around with, especially in combination with other written words.

To this end it is highly recommended that you spend some time every day playing around with written words yourself. This can be with no particular goal or project in mind, and can indeed consist of writing absolute gobbledegook. What matters is that you set up a daily channel for written words to come through you. To facilitate this, all you need is a pen-paper/keyboard-mouse situation happening and away you go. Write down whatever comes into your head. Don't be shy, self-critical, or self-censorious and feel free to write the biggest lot of bollocks imaginable.

Simply write down the chatter/imaginary dialogue occurring in your head. Give yourself at least two pages of space to express yourself on, and don't bother reading it till much later (unless it's good). After five weeks of this, read over what you've done, extract all the good/coherent/interesting/poetic/unusual bits and chunk them altogether and you may find you've got the makings of a plot or a philosophical treatise.

Or you may not.

Naming your project/self

There is a given name for every project/product, all you have to do is discover what it is. You don't have to make a name up. It already exists in the ether of your unconscious mind. All you have to do is ask your higher self/unconscious mind to furnish your conscious mind/local self with the information you need, and then wait. The name will come to you during a dream, or on the side of a passing van. If not, and you've got to the project's completion and it's time to present it to the world, you can always use the 'Two Dogs Fucking' method, as in, 'Dad, how did you come up with my name?' 'I went out in the yard straight after you were born, and named you after the first thing I saw. Why do you ask, Two Dogs Fucking?' Old gag,

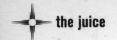

but good method if you're stuck for the odd moniker.

Talking of which, you might want to consider the possible advantages of using an alias or series of aliases for yourself. This gives you an unlimited amount of attention-attracting and intriguing titles to choose from or concoct.

Moreover, as well as providing you with a safe form of expression for any latent schizophrenia, it also provides you with an alternative real-life character to explore. Because once an alias is established, the character attached to it takes on a persona and flavour all of its own, which may be subtly or even grossly different from the one associated with the name on your birth certificate. Creating an alias is symbolic of reinventing yourself, which is often the appropriate/expedient next move to make, both from a marketing perspective and from the point of view of living your living theatre more fully [see *Living theatre* p.40].

Writing

The ability to express your ideas clearly in written word is almost essential, no matter which other art form/s you specialise in.

Most projects involve writing proposals.

Most projects involve writing press releases/ad-slogans/buy-lines/business plans, etc.

Most projects involve written instructions for others to follow.

Most projects involve writing business letters and e-mails.

Obviously, the more adroit you become at expressing yourself in written word, the more easily others will understand your wishes, which increases the odds for your wishes being fulfilled (on all levels).

EXCELLENCE NUMBER FIVE: PRESENTATION SKILLS (FIRE ELEMENT)

Traditionally, this is calligraphy and/or playing a musical instrument. Presentation describes that point of interface between your product and the market place which occurs the moment the finished article is revealed to an intermediary and/or to the end-user, i.e. your public/the audience/the punter.

Packaging, in other words. This may be in the form of a solid object (book/CD/shirt/dress/Aston Martin, etc.), a performance (film, stage-play, concert, etc.), or a service (healing/teaching/lecture/consultancy/ training, etc.).

It is the point at which your product/self, i.e. your message-carrier ceases to be private/personal and becomes public property (however briefly), the point at which your product makes its presence felt.

Presentation skills comprise your ability to bring the presence of your product/self to bear on the prevailing culture with enough impact to make a positive upwards difference to your bank balance. When bringing your product to market, you are bringing yourself with it, i.e. to promote your product you will hopefully be required to talk about it/you on TV and radio, as well as speaking about it/yourself in print, for which you may also be photographed. Additionally, you may be required to provide publicity shots of yourself, or produce promotional videos/TV/radio programme pilots. So as well as attending to the presentation of your product, whether it be a book, record, show, film or whatever, you must also attend to the presentation of yourself.

Self-presentation

As a living art form, you impact on others (in the living theatre – your audience) in the following ways:

Sight Your external appearance/image: your posture, physical shape, facial features, hair, clothes and shoes, in movement and at rest (all of it, not just the shoes), impacts upon others by providing information about you which supports your message/product more or less convincingly/synergistically [see *Style* p.197].

Sound Unless you're a professional purveyor of music/song or/and a tap-dancer/handclapping flamenco dancer, your sonic impact on others is mostly limited to the sound of your spoken voice, acts of loudly passing wind, inadvertent or otherwise, through mouth or anus notwithstanding.

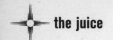

Smell Apart from those times when, for reasons of your own, you go without attending to personal hygiene for an extended period, are suffering from incontinence and/or uncontrollable vomiting, gangrene, or are simply dead and rotting in the open, your impact on the olfactory experience of others is mostly caused by the perfume you wear and the various perfumes contained in your shampoo/conditioner/soap/deodorant/face-cream, etc., as well as the odour of any smoke whether tobacco, cannabis, or incense, which you cause to be habitually burning in close proximity to your person.

Touch Your impact on other people's sense of touch occurs on hand-shaking, kissing, hugging, healing, fighting, crashing into them while operating a vehicle, bumping into them in the street/bar, falling on them from a high place, and making love/doing sex with them.

Taste (sometimes) The impact you have on someone's tastebuds, other than when you prepare/buy them a meal or drink is limited to those times when you French-kiss them, they perform oral sex on you, lick you, or in any other way gain access to the way you taste including those times (that time) you inadvertently give yourself up for cannibalisation.

If you wish to optimise on the positive effects of your physical impact on others, both for them, and for the sake of the impression you leave, there are various things which can be done.

Visual impact

The face you show the world can be beautiful; the skin can be tightened, muscle tone improved, circulation increased and eyes brightened in the following ways.

Stretching These moves must be performed indoors both to prevent your face getting stuck in the wind, i.e. windstroke, and other people pointing:

> *Elongate your face by simultaneously stretching your chin towards the floor and your forehead towards the ceiling.*

Shorten your face by drawing all your features towards the tip of your nose, i.e. scrunch up your face.

Alternate these two eighteen times, luxuriating in the stretch and relishing the feeling of releasing facial tension.

Rotate your chin like a camel chewing, as if wiping a window with your chin in small circular movements (rotations), eighteen times counter-clockwise and eighteen times clockwise.

Rotate the tip of your tongue so it rubs in circles round the outside of your gums, eighteen times counter-clockwise and eighteen times clockwise.

Gently knock your upper and lower teeth together thirty-six times.

Self-massage Place your palms on your face, one on either side of your nose. Massage (stroke) with four ounces of pressure upwards over the forehead. Separate your palms to the sides of your forehead and stroke down the sides of your face to start the cycle again. Repeat this eighteen times.

Make fists and use your knuckles gently to percuss (bang) all over your skull, back, sides, top and forehead, for about ninety seconds. (Keep your shoulders relaxed.)

Place a middle finger on the bone at the outer corner of each eye. Gently, so as not to burn or over-stretch the skin, massage/stroke inwards along the bone under each eye towards the inner corner of each eye.

Now stroke along the bone running over each eye to the outer-corner of each eye. Repeat this movement eighteen times.

Rub lightly but briskly in small up and down sandpapering-like movements all over the face.

Eyes These movements must be performed slowly without effort or strain to prevent the retina from detaching itself.

To brighten your eyes, as well as strengthen the eye muscles, look straight up and down nine times.

Rest your palms over your eyes for a moment.

Look from side to side nine times. Rest as before.

Look from top left corner to bottom right corner nine times. Rest.

Look from top right corner to bottom left nine times. Rest.

Circle your eyes once counter-clockwise and once clockwise. Rest.

Personal hygiene

Maintain cleanliness of all hair, skin, cracks, orifices, nails, teeth, and any other permanent or semi-permanent appendages and attachments, organic or otherwise (clothing, footwear, false teeth, and limbs, wigs and hairpieces, spectacles/contact lenses and hearing aids, colostomy bags, etc.), associated with your physical person on a daily basis.

Perfume

Your perfume (including all applied scents) must not be so strong or liberally applied that it telegraphs your arrival (they shouldn't be able to smell you coming) but must be strong enough to leave a subtle pleasing after-trace when you've gone. Perfume is there to sweeten the atmosphere of your up-close, immediate vicinity, i.e. your personal, intimate space, for the potential benefit of those with whom you share that space (mostly yourself and your lovers).

Perfume is not intended for use as an olfactory protective force field.

In other words, avoid using scents in such abundance or of such inherent strength that you overwhelm/invade other people with them.

Perfume is intended to mix with and enhance the natural scents produced by the internal chemistry of your body, and not as a way of masking smells you're ashamed of. If your body is producing smells like that, it's indicative of imbalance and possibly disease. If this persists, consider visiting an experienced, authentic healer/doctor for examination of internal organ functions. (This applies also to excessive use of breath-freshener to mask bad breath.)

Clothing and hairstyle

The tidiness, cleanliness and aesthetic cultural/social aptness of your clothes, shoes, (nails) and hairstyle, i.e. that which is attached to your physical person in such a way that it can be removed at any time without causing physical pain to your person, and comprising the aspects of your physical appearance most suceptible/available to sudden change, must be attended to with enough application and regularity that you don't feel you have to hide bits of yourself or in any way alter or inhibit your range of physical movement in public.

In other words, pay enough attention to your appearance without giving way to obsessiveness [see *Vanity* p.78], so that when you step out of your house/dressing room into public domain, you don't have to think/worry about other people thinking you're dirty, smelly, impoverished, unkempt, uncared for, unsuccessful and above all unself-respecting.

Obviously, with enough conviction and talent you can get a record deal/publishing deal, attend business meetings, perform on stage or TV, or attend the premiere of your new movie with sick all down your front, a split in your pants and holes in your trainers – but why make it more difficult than you have to?

Movement, posture and grace

The way you move and the way you hold yourself determines the quality of response others have to your physical presence.

Stand, sit and walk with dignity and grace like a leopard. Relaxed, natural uprightness of posture, will make people treat you with respect.

Stand, sit and walk with shame like a wretched, self-conscious cur, head bowed over a crumpled torso, and people will walk all over you.

To rectify your posture in order to maximise on public impact, partake of regular training in martial arts, intelligent weight-work, yoga, Alexander Technique, and/or any combination of the above.

Sonic impact

Read a newspaper or watch the news on TV.

Other than at times of extreme catastrophic upheaval (earthquakes, world wars, royal weddings/divorces/funerals, at least half, if not two-thirds of items covered on a daily basis concern words people have spoken. The prime minister said this. The president said that. The mistress said this. The terrorist leader said that.

Words have power. They carry information in a most elaborate way. But because we get so used to them, we forget to appreciate the range of complex physical and intellectual factors involved every time one person speaks to another, both in the talking and the listening/understanding processes.

However, intellectual content is only a small percentage of the message carried in your words. Consider the absolute crap spoken by the majority of those in the news most of the time and this becomes obvious. But they get away with it. You actually listen to what they're telling you even when you know it's bullshit.

Why?

Because, apart from their conviction and intention of being strong enough to carry their message, you more or less like the actual sound of their voice.

The sound of your voice is even more important than the quality and/or content of your words. Which is not to advocate that you aspire to feeding the world loads of shit and getting away with it just because they like the tone and timbre of your voice and the fact that you've kept all your cracks and orifices clean as above. But that if you do, at least make sure it sounds good to the ear (for everyone's sake).

Your speaking voice is a musical instrument which, if played correctly, will carry your spoken message into the hearts of whoever's listening.

To develop and hone your playing, that is to improve/deepen the tone and timbre of your voice, thus making it easier to project effectively, look at the following on a daily or bi-daily basis:

Vocal training

Your skull acts as a resonance chamber. To increase resonance levels in your skull and thereby increase the richness and puissance of your speaking voice, do this:

Humming exercise:

Take a fat (phat) breath in. On the out-breath, hum the sound 'mmmmmmmm-mmmmmmmmmmmmm'. Feel it vibrate in your cheekbones, around your eyes and across your forehead.

Take a fat (phat) breath in. On the out-breath, go, 'meemeemeemee-meemeemeemeemeemeemeemee'. Then, 'mamamamamamamamamamamama-mamamam', and so on through all the vowel sounds, short, long and twisted, as in, 'ai, ah, eh, ee, o, oh, oi, u, ooo', etc. Feel the sound vibrating all through the front of your face.

Repeat this same process with 'n', this time feeling the vibration up your nose and in your sinuses.

Now repeat using 'ng' as in king, feeling the vibration in the back of your skull.

As well as increasing resonance, humming in this fashion is a marvellous way to clear your head in the morning (afternoon and suppertime), and is strongly recommended as preparation for meditation.

Sliding exercise:

To give your voice more dynamic range, i.e. rise and fall, and thus inject a mesmerising musical quality into your words, so preventing too much monotony creeping into your sentences, do this:

Take a deep, fat (phat) breath in. As you breathe out, make the sound 'ah' in as high (falsetto) a note as you can, letting it slide slowly down the register until it ends just before your breath runs out at the deepest note you can make. As the sound descends through the scale from high to low, visualise it sliding down the front of your body from your forehead to your pubic bone.

Repeat the slide making the sounds, 'ai, ee, eh, o, oh, oo, uh'.

Short slide:

Take a deep, fat breath in, and make the sound, 'eeeeeeeeyyoh', starting high (falsetto) and ending deep (bass). Visualise the sound sliding quickly down the front of your body as before.

Importance of breathing in speech production

Always ensure adequate breath supplies are available to support the

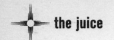

sound of your voice. Talking on empty lungs is like trying to get a sound out of a saxophone without blowing it.

Always allow enough of a pause between phrases, i.e. at the commas, to enable you to refill your lungs. Pausing for breath will not make you lose your listener's attention. To the contrary, it allows them time to absorb what you're saying.

Focusing on the breath like this while engaged in conversation/public speaking/presenting/acting etc., turns talking into a meditation and makes your daily experience of living theatre more complete [see *Living theatre* p.40].

For eight days, make a point of taking extra-long in-breaths before each new phrase you utter to others and simply observe what occurs during that pause, both within you and in the behaviour of the listener.

Note: it is inadvisable to indulge in the making of funny/self-conscious/strange faces or grinning inanely during such pauses, as this will induce ICR (instant credibility reduction).

Microphone technique

First, acquaint yourself with the pick-up zone/sound-catchment area of the microphone you're using. This is usually facilitated by listening carefully to on-stage monitors, studio headphones or if engaged in public speaking without the benefit of on-stage monitors, to the sound coming through to the audience, and is effected by shifting your mouth nearer and further from the microphone while making vocal sounds such as 'one two one two' in a pre-gig sound-check situation, or while saying the opening words of your speech, where no previous sound-check has been possible.

It is always better to start off further back than further forward, i.e. too quiet rather than too loud, to avoid the listener suffering sonic shock. Always watch out for popping caused by the plosive sounds, 'b' and 'p'. To help minimise popping, practice the following exercise:

Take a deep breath in and without moving your mouth, simply allowing your lips to flap, make the sound, 'beepah beepah beepah beepah'. Hold your palm up in front of your mouth to ascertain relative velocity levels of the air escaping from your mouth as you make the sound. You should be able to feel no breath hitting your palm, while making 'beepah' as loud as you can.

Once you feel comfortable with your distance from the microphone, and are happy with the sound of your voice [see *Vocal training* p.186] coming through the monitors, imagine that the mike is merely an extension of your body. Forget it's there and act naturally. (And speak up!)

Claiming the space

When you get up on stage, or into the recording booth, or walk into the meeting/presentation/pitch, before doing anything else, claim the space as your own. Simply say to yourself by way of reminding yourself, 'I deserve to be here. Wherever I am is my space. I now claim this space as my own!' You can also try saying it out loud for experimental purposes only, if you do it with enough conviction and think you'll get away with it.

Telephone technique

When, using a mobile or fixed-line, non-video, audio-only phone, you call someone on business or for something important, where you care about the outcome of the call, be aware that:

You have no idea what state of mind and mood that person on the other end will be in.

You have no idea of the events which led up to that person taking your call.

Without knowing what mood or condition you'll find that person in, your intention is to gain instant access to one of that person's most intimate and well-guarded areas – the inside of his/her brain.

To thus enter someone's brain through their ear telephonically therefore requires that you pay extra attention to breathing and voice sound (depth, resonance, tone, pitch and timbre), because in this instance, your voice is the only way you have to convey information. That person cannot see your involuntary facial expressions or body language, which normally carry ninety-one per cent of your message.

Your goal is to massage that person's body from the inside using the vibrations in your voice. Once this internal massage process has kicked

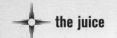

in, usually some time during the hello-how-are-you phase, you can then proceed to deliver the content. When doing so, however, be sure to inject adequate amounts of chi (energy) [see *Meditation* p.126] to infuse your vocal sound with enough enthusiasm, confidence or whichever emotion is appropriate to the situation, to make you sound convincing.

To effect this, simply think about your 'tan tien' two thumb-widths down and in from your navel, while you both speak and listen. This will keep you centred and in touch with your own feelings as they shift according to how the conversation's going. Remaining centred affords you both the patience to listen to what that person has to say and the clarity to think about how you wish to respond.

Don't be afraid of pauses. Use all pauses to breathe and wait until the conversation picks up on its own, from your end or theirs, or dwindles to an obvious cut-off point. Relish the pauses, however temporarily uncomfortable they might be. In the pauses you will find the Tao. And that's when the magic begins.

And if none of that works and you still don't get what you think you want out of them, say goodbye politely, put the phone down and say 'fuck 'em!' [see *Just say 'fuck 'em* p.104].

Becoming fluent in body language

Warning! Karma hazard – avoid using to manipulate others.

When your surrounding energy field/aura/charisma is strong, i.e. positively charged, people respond to you in positive ways and are more open to giving you what you want (if you know what that is).

The practice of meditation and martial arts develops and reinforces your energy field, and comes highly recommended.

However, to maintain this in public situations when having to engage in social or professional intercourse of any kind while not simultaneously engaged in the practice of meditation or martial arts, you are advised to remain mindful of keeping your body posture open.

When your posture is closed, cramped, or diminished in any way, especially around the armpits, between the legs, around the anus/rectum, hands, feet or forehead, you're blocking the flow or fluency of chi and your energy field/charisma will be proportionately diminished.

Always allow the language of your body to be fluent.

In all public situations, check in with your body at regular intervals.

First, always check that you're breathing, i.e. not holding your breath. Second, check your armpits. If your armpits are open, with enough space to fit a small golden apple, your shoulders and chest will drop and your upper energy field will intensify. Third, check between your legs. If your gential region is relaxed, your sexual energy can flow more freely, lending an extra air of attractiveness to your person. Fourth, check your anus/rectum region. If your anus is relaxed, your energy can circulate more freely. You become less anal. If that and your genitals are relaxed, your lower energy field will be intensified. Fifth, check your hands, feet and forehead. If your extremities are relaxed your entire upper and lower energy field will be intensified, and you'll be shining like a star. Only cross your arms when you actively wish to protect yourself against someone's negative energy. Otherwise, remain as physically open as you can, with palms facing whoever you're talking to.

Being thus sensitive to how your own energy field opens up and closes down according to your posture, and noticing that when you close down it's because your're hiding something (fear/anger/shyness/distaste, etc.), you become equally as sensitive to what's going on with someone else.

In other words, get fluent in your own body language and you'll notice more clearly and quickly when someone's not being fluent in theirs. Knowing how someone's blocking, and therefore finding energetic ways round those blocks, may help you communicate more effectively with them.

Buy a book on body language (it'll only take you ten minutes to get the basic formula) and start noticing what goes on between you and others on that level of communication which, as I said, is where, along with smell, etc. at least ninety-one per cent of information is carried between people. (IWT statistics.).

Importance of visual presentation

Originally/traditionally, practitioners of the Five Excellences, and in particular the Excellence of effective visual presentation, thought in terms of calligraphy.

Calligraphy, at that time, was the only way of conveying written information. The Taoist tradition of calligraphic practices emphasises the internal psycho-energetic condition of the practitioner as much as, if not even more than, the finished product of that practitioner's doings.

When approaching the blank paper/parchment, brush/quill-pen in hand, the focus is on the 'tan tien' (two thumb-widths down and in from the navel – how many more times?!), and on the absolute unity of artist, brush/quill-pen, paper/parchment and the Tao/higher self.

Then, with the intended result held just behind the centre of the forehead, brush/quill-pen and parchment meet as if of themselves and without conscious interference by the artist, between them materialise whichever shape/pattern arises as if from the Tao, according to the artist's original intention. And hey presto you've got a piece/product/pure information-carrier.

In contemporary terms, calligraphy equates to graphic design. Graphic design is currently one of the most (if not most) prevalent art forms on the planet.

Graphic design infiltrates your consciousness at every turn. Consider all the products you consume or would like to consume. Consider all the other products you wouldn't like to consume, but others would and do. Put all these products together. (Product includes all art forms, services, governmental/infrastructural institutions, media, etc.) Think globally. That's a lot of products.

Graphic design is employed for the logo, name, and other symbols/slogans/images which establish and reinforce brand identity, in the packaging, promotion and advertising of each of those products.

Remember that advertising includes adverts in newspapers and magazines, on billboards, on the Internet, on TV, in the cinema, on the side of delivery vehicles, at point of sale within stores, and on the product itself, as on the outside of clothing and footwear for example.

Consider the volume of graphic information on a global scale of all the packaging and advertising of all the products in existence, and add to that all the street signs, traffic signs and any other example of graphic display you can think of, where it says volume on your stereo, police on the side of a police car, telephone above a public telephone, as well as exit signs in theatres, supermarkets, car parks, airport lounges, computer programs and then add to that all the packaging of all the products in all the shops, stores, supermarkets, gas stations, superstores ... is it starting to make you feel nauseous yet?

Graphic design touches on your consciousness (and more insidiously, your unconsciousness) at every moment of your day/night. Unless you're up in some cave somewhere being holy. And even then you must have a watch or pair of trainers.

For this reason, when launching/relaunching a product/message/ reinvented version of yourself, you must pay strong attention to the visual presentation aspects of your product, all the way through from letterheads and business cards and flyers to adverts on billboards, the Internet and TV.

The stronger your visual brand identity, i.e. logo, name, slogans and other associated images (as well as the way these are laid out), the more easily your product will be recognised and accepted by market-place intermediaries and finally your potential punters.

Work on constantly improving your visual brand image. Simply allow it to evolve in your mind and translate 'pen-ually' to paper as it evolves.

Contemporary 'calligraphy' employs keyboard, mouse, scanner and screen instead of brush, quill, ink and parchment, but the principles of practice are the same. When approaching your computer, do so thinking of your 'tan tien' (no, I'm not going to say it again!), and with your intended result held firmly but lightly just behind the centre of your forehead, your mind empty [see *Meditation* p.126] and your countenance all aglow (from the glare of the screen!), put your hand on the mouse and let the Tao take over.

Make liberal use of your scanner to scan in organically sourced material, i.e. not digitally generated, in order to perpetuate general recycling of images, and because it looks fresher and more original. Even if you employ the services of or work alongside a graphic designer, it is important to be conversant enough with the graphic design process and language to be able to know and communicate what kind of image you're after, and then to recognise it when you see it. (So you can go, 'Great! Wicked! Fabulous!', as you walk into the design studio to see what they've done for you so far.)

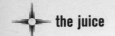

Importance of having a good tool

While it's true that many of the greatest creative contributions to our culture, in all fields of artistic endeavour, are made by equipmentally challenged artists, and while it's also empirically and undeniably true that a bad workman always blames his/her tool/s, it doesn't half help to have a good tool.

Whenever possible, always make sure you have the right tool to do the job at hand. Always, within reason, keep your tools clean and in good working order. Spend regular time engaged in tool maintenance activities and never begrudge time, energy or money spent on such maintenance, repair and replacement, and upgrade as is necessary to keep you in the game.

Tools include all equipment, props, substances and materials you need to fulfil your function as artist-practitioner in your chosen field/s of endeavour. Singers use microphones and glycerine. DJs use vinyl records, CDs, tapes, headphones and turntables. Musicians use instruments, amplification and effect units, leads, reeds, skins, sticks, computers, recording studios, etc. Painters use brushes, rollers, paint, canvas, easels, etc. Graphic designers use computers, scanners, printers, colour photocopiers and so on.

Treat your tools with love and respect, as you would any friend upon whom you rely. Allow your energy to suffuse every tool you use. Let your tool/s be an extension of your physical body. When using any tool/piece of equipment, think about your 'tan tien' and let there be a mental connection between it and the tool you're using.

Musical instruments, recording studios (the Tao of sound)

Traditionally, presentational skills included the ability to play a musical instrument. This pretty much limited the old Taoists of yore to the pippa (lute), bamboo flute, human singing voice and various percussion instruments and drums.

No matter the paucity of choice, the artist (musician) would approach his/her instrument thinking about his/her 'tan tien' and holding the clear intent to produce sound of the highest quality, would project his/her chi (energy) into the instrument so it became an extension of his/her body and with an empty mind [see *Meditation* p.126] would lose him/herself in the Tao and let the instrument play itself.

Rather than striving for virtuosity or perfect technique, the artist strives to make each note sound with perfect tone. By focusing on the quality of each note, each note becomes a timeless celebration of the Tao, and as such, when run in sequence with all the other notes in the tune, creates an alchemical synergy whereby the whole is far greater than the sum of its parts.

In other words, shut up and play the tune.

In contemporary terms, this means that when you approach your microphone, piano, keyboard, violin, electric guitar, horn, saxophone, entire recording studio, approach with the intention to celebrate the particular vibrational quality, clarity, purity, timbre, tone and pitch of every note and noise you make. Then, thinking of your 'tan tien', become one with the instrument and one with the Tao and let the music make itself. The inclusion of an entire recording studio in the above list of musical instruments is intentional. In contemporary music-making, a producer/artist in his/her studio is the modern-day equivalent of an old Taoist hero with his/her bamboo flute. This also applies to DJs who, when playing other people's tunes, are in fact using those tunes as source material to create a sound of their own, by subjecting them to scratching, mixing and EQ-rearrangement processes at the decks, i.e. the decks become the instrument and the tune becomes the individual notes, each one of which must ring out with clarity, quality and power. (DJ Tan Tien!)

Developing a healthy relationship with the camera lens (still and moving)

When you look at the camera lens forget about the photographer, forget about yourself. Think about your 'tan tien' and imagine that the lens is the eyes of someone who really loves you, totally approves of you, thinks you're totally sexy, beautiful, charming, handsome/pretty, desirable, irresistible, interesting, riveting and generally magnificent. Imagine you're in dialogue with that person and simply let your physical person express to the lens the feelings that occur around your 'tan tien'.

If you don't resonate with that, imagine the lens is the eye of the Tao,

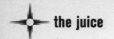

your personal god/goddess, or your own higher self. (However, this tends to make you look a bit glassy-eyed.)

This merging with the camera gets easier with practice, until eventually you forget the camera, the camera operator and yourself. Just don't forget your lines.

To reinforce the you-camera-Tao merging process say, 'I love to see the camera lens, gazing at my face; I see it as my loving friend from the camera-headed-race.'

Importance of lighting and angle

Your experience of a situation is determined by the angle from which you're viewing it and by the way the scene is lit. Similarly, the way others see you depends on the angle from which they're looking and the way you've been lit. This applies whether viewing you through the naked eye or through the lens of a camera, and also applies to when they look at your image on still or moving film.

That's why someone looks beautiful to you one moment and damn rough the next. It's all to do with camera angle lighting.

Do everything you can to ensure that you're being lit sympathetically and viewed from the optimum angle whenever you find yourself on stage or in front of a camera. Do not be obsessive about this, however. It's perfectly fine and inevitable to be seen and be filmed/photographed looking ugly from time to time.

Knowing this helps you see through the illusion of living theatre [see *Living theatre* p.40], helps you see behind people's masks and can be used too, from time to time, to show yourself to your best advantage in certain social, professional or creative situations. Whenever staging an event in public, always pay abundant attention to both stage and ambient lighting, as well as visual projections and backdrops, for maximum alchemical effect, i.e. never treat lighting as a low priority. Lighting can make or break an event. (Let there be light.) This also applies to the lighting in your workplace and home.

On attaining cultural relevance

Do not be overly concerned with your art being culturally relevant. In this cut'n'paste culture, everything is relevant, i.e. usable/reusable. It's all in how you present it. Watch a bit of TV, especially MTV every now and then, listen to a smattering of radio, look in a few culture/style magazines from time to time, but generally carry on focusing on doing your art in your way and, if you keep producing and showing, producing and showing, eventually the world will come to you.

Trust that. Trying to follow and cater to the fickleness of 'public' taste and changing trends is like trying to lick your own bum.

Write down fifty-two times (one for each week of the year), 'Everything I produce is relevant to my culture. I am relevant to my culture. And why? Because I say so!'

Importance of editing

No matter what medium you're working in, whether it's sound, vision, literature, performance, theatre, dance, film, journalism, etc., when it comes to presenting the finished product, an effective editing process is essential.

It's not what you say, show, play, write or sing that makes the piece complete, it's what you don't.

It's the spaces between the notes that let you hear the notes. It's the action you don't see in the play or movie that gets your imagination going. It's the things you don't say in the story that provide the spaces between the lines for you to read.

Never shy away from a ruthless edit session. If the material still stands up, it's a product. If not it'll show you clearly which bits need attention.

(I wonder if this item will survive the edit?)

Style

Style comes from being practical about your needs and requirements, and imaginative in the way you set about fulfilling them.

Style does not come from attempting to be stylish. That just makes you look like someone attempting to be stylish.

Style is always original because it arises from following an inner vision rather than following what someone else is doing/wearing, etc. Style shows up in the way you dress and do your hair, the equipment you use, the chattels you possess, the food, drink and substances you consume, the

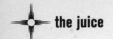

way you entertain yourself, the place you live in, the place you work in, the way you transport yourself between these and other destinations, the other places you visit and (in case I've forgotten anything) the way you're seen to spend your time.

Style arises as a symptom of your practical nature and creative imagination. The fact that other people think of you as having or not having style is their business, not yours.

You like to sleep on a futon on the floor because you like sleeping on a hard surface. You roll it up in the daytime because you like to use the room for other things too. You see no reason why a room must be designated for bed use only, just because that's what most people do. You do this because you're practical about your needs concerning beds and room-space and because you have the imagination not simply to follow others if their ways don't suit your requirements.

A journalist friend who writes for an interior-design publication comes to visit and likes the way you use the space. She likes it because you have style and whatever you do looks good. (From your point of view you're just doing it because that's what you do.) Next month, the magazine she's on runs a feature on the way people are rolling up their futons these days, a couple of Sunday newspapers pick up on it and run rolled-up futon articles in their leisure pages, and suddenly everyone's buying futons and rolling them up all over the place because it's stylish. (Wait till you start sleeping on a bamboo mat!)

For you, it has nothing to do with style. It's simply a matter of practicality. Style, i.e. practicality plus imagination, is symptomatic of your innate ability to make the best of your available resources by being clear about your actual needs, rather than thinking you need things just because other people think *they* need them, and has nothing to do with how much or how little money you have.

Marketing and cross-marketing

Marketing is simply that process whereby you bring your product to the market place, whence it can be disseminated for popular use.

In the old days people would bring their produce to market and all business transactions would be conducted there. This held true whether you were a farmer selling your cow, a cabinet maker selling your cabinet or a minstrel looking for a gig. The market place today, rather than being concentrated in the town square, is spread out all over the globe, with points of access afforded at various key points mostly in major metropolitan regions.

Other than for meetings, professional engagements and networking activities, the market place is usually entered by remote access, i.e. by phone/Internet/e-mail/fax/postal service, etc. Your point of contact with the market place may be an agent, manager, publishing company, record company, magazine publisher, distributor, wholesaler, manufacturer, etc.

Do not be afraid to enter the market place [see *Dealing with fear of rejection/humiliation* p.100]. The market place is always hungry for new products, no matter the prevailing economic climate. The worst that can happen is you get told to fuck off and that won't kill you [see *Just say 'fuck 'em!'* p.104].

Cross-marketing is when you get one product to promote another. Examples of this are the tops of the containers for Chinese take-away food advertising videos; placement of recognisable branded goods in movies; billboards advertising insurance companies on televised sports events; an author's second book advertising his/her first book on its rear cover, and so on.

Cross-marketing is getting one product to ride on the back of another with the intended synergistic effect of *both* products selling in increased volume. Take advantage of as many cross-marketing opportunities as you can. This is similar to sending your message through as many carriers as you can.

You write a best-selling book. You record a CD of tunes. You promote the record on the back of your reputation as an author. The record charts. You bring out a perfume line and promote on the back of your reputation as an author and tunesmith. Now every time someone goes past your perfume at the duty-free, it reinforces your brand identity in their mind, so that the next time they read a review of your book or CD they'll be more inclined to give it a whirl. And if they do, the chances are that next time they fly, they'll probably buy the perfume too. And so on until

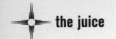

product by product you eventually take over the entire world! (Quick, come and take him away!)

Importance of PR (perception management)

The function of public relations is to establish your presence or the presence of your product in the public's mind, via the offices of receptive/ sympathetic/eager-for-a-story journalist/reviewers/critics/gossip columnists (mongerers) across as many different media as possible, thereafter discreetly to manage public perception of you and/or your product, including the employment of damage-limitation tactics where appropriate, in as best way they can, circumstances and budget permitting.

A campaign to promote a new product usually spans a three-month period, involving the composition of a viable and enticing press release and associated gimmicks such as innovative free giveaways, the sending out of that press release to all relevant parties, following that up with the phone calls, the arranging of interviews and TV/radio chat shows and promotional public appearances (shopping malls etc.), arranging a launch party/event inviting the 'right' guests, talking it up (you/the product) at other parties and social events to instigate a word of mouth process (WOMP) and generally enthusing about you/the product to anyone who'll listen.

This costs money. You could do it all yourself but then you wouldn't have time to get on with your work. As it is when you have a new product to promote, it can be a near full-time occupation for the period of time involved, while you go from chat show to chat show, interview to interview and so on.

Media exposure received as a result of a successful PR campaign is far more effective and usually reaches and convinces far more people than straightforward advertising, and is relatively far cheaper (pro rata to the results in increased sales). This works on the basis that people are much more likely to believe in your product if someone else other than you, i.e. your advert, tells them to. Especially if that someone is writing in a newspaper/magazine or talking on TV/radio. Because even though people know what a grand illusion the media generates, they still allow themselves to be influenced. (It must be true, I saw it on TV/read it in the paper.) This is made possible, as is all illusion, by the highly developed human talent for self-deception, as well as a willingness to be a good sport.

For this reason, PR is worth every penny you invest or equally every hour you spend (if you're doing it yourself).

sentimental

outro

DEALING WITH THE PRESSURE

When it all kicks in and you've got one product coming out in one country, another somewhere else, the previous one selling and spin-off products about to launch, and your PR person wants to speak to you, and your agent wants a meeting, your manager needs to speak to you and your accountant rings and you need to phone the travel agent and pay the phone bill and buy the food for dinner and you've got to do a chat show appearance and everyone needs you *now*, and you have to start work on your next project in order to meet your deadline, *and* your lover/partner/spouse is complaining that you don't spend enough time with him/her/the family, and you know you need to spend more time practising your martial arts and meditation ... wait! Did you say martial arts and meditation?

When the pressure builds up it is more important than ever to build in regular meditation and martial arts training periods into your daily schedule and to exercise self-discipline to follow through with it, during which sacred time the whole world can go fuck itself. Moreover, you must ensure adequate sleep time is secured on a daily basis. Maintain as well balanced a diet as you can manage, get outside as often as possible, eschew the use of artificial stimulants (cocaine, speed, alcohol, pain-killers) to keep you going as much as possible, turn off your mobile and/or fixed-line phone as often as possible, pray a lot and above all, *breathe*!

Knowing when to beat a retreat/retire/make a comeback

Sometimes you may find it expedient to beat a hasty/expedient retreat from the glare of the market place and public gaze.

Reasons you may wish to do this:

The pressure of market place/public demand is too great for even Tai Chi to be of any help; you're bored; you need to go into seclusion to work on your next project; you/your product has reached market saturation levels and you/your advisers reckon you need some time out to reinvent; you need a vacation; you've had enough, or whatever.

It is always useful to know/have access to/own somewhere you can

retreat to, which is far enough away and inaccessible enough to deter a
but those you specifically invite to join you from pitching up unexpec
edly, and yet close and accessible enough for you to get to without to
much time or trouble, and which is adequately linked by digital commu
nication systems to enable you to remain in touch via e-mail
telephone/TV as and when you wish.

This may occur at times when you still have commitments and projec
pending and are therefore obliged to make it a temporary retreat, or
may occur when you have no further projects in sight and no more con
mitments to fulfil and have reached a temporary/permanent creativ
hiatus.

At these times (financial position permitting), you may wish to exten
your retreat indefinitely, i.e. retire. If, after some time, you decide to sta
out of the game for good, read a few books, walk, watch a bit of telly
devote some time to your martial arts, meditation and spiritual develop
ment, maybe teach a few young ones, spend a bit of time with you
family, lover, partner, spouse or friends, maybe travel a bit, that's up t
you and good luck to ye.

If, on the other hand, your creative juices start flowing again and yo
find yourself getting drawn inexorably back into composition and pr
duction mode, or if it's simply that your money runs out, you may fin
yourself compelled to make a comeback. If so, and your motivations ar
pure, you're speaking your truth and still have the knack of shaping it a
into some kind of relevant message, your return will be like that of th
prodigal son/daughter and will afford you a most magnificent opportu
nity for personal development and living-theatre-style entertainment. C
it may just be a flop. (How would *I* know!)

Short-term it is always good policy to beat a temporary retreat for u
to a month or so, every three of four months. This will provide you wit
time for creating and recreating, i.e. recreation which is vital to th
ongoing status of your person. It has the added benefit of keeping yo
fresh in the minds of those you work with on a regular basis. It give
them a chance to miss you and prevents you being around long enoug
in any one place to get on people's nerves.

What to do with fame and fortune once you've got it?

Enjoy it,

(you fool!!!)

Dealing with the fear of loss

Every night before sleep and every morning after awakening, remind yourself that in reality you possess nothing except what you're left with after you've died. (That's right, not even your body!)

Accept that.

Breathe.

Reflect on all you own/possess, including all monies owing to you. Realise that it's all bunce (bonus). Say thank you to the Tao/your higher self/God or whatever you believe in at that moment.

Realise that in reality you have nothing to lose.

Breathe.

Trust that your survival needs will always be met until the moment you die.

Continue with your life.

Alternatively, become anxious, paranoid and insecure, make silly decisions and start driving yourself and everyone around you round the bend.

The importance of keeping your overheads down

Resist all temptations to spend more than you're earning.

Resist all temptations to build yourself an edifice or install yourself in grandiose, high-rent, high-upkeep headquarters. It impresses no one but the stupid and uninformed.

Resist all temptations to commit yourself to spending money you haven't got or have no way as yet of earning.

Resist all temptations to buy on credit and notch up huge monthly payments.

Resist all temptations to take on a large mortgage or bank loan to pay for a piece of real estate which might cause you to be placed in negative equity status when values depreciate or the market crashes.

Resist all temptations to take on a mortgage at all if you can help it,

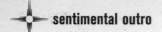

preferring to rent/squat/camp-out/stay on the move until such time as you can go into the house shop and buy one outright.

Resist all temptations to take on a permanent staff whom you are obliged to keep paying even when you haven't got the money coming in

Resist all temptations. (Just kidding.)

Maintain your fixed costs at the lowest possible level, making use of short-term rental and employment arrangements as and when you need to or whenever possible, in order to enable you to relocate temporarily or permanently with relative ease and speed, should conditions so demand.

This doesn't mean being mean. Be abundantly generous to yourself and others, but be prudent with your resources.

Keeping current

Avoid allowing a backlog to build up of project work to be completed, bills to pay, debts to repay, correspondence to deal with, phone calls to make, equipment maintenance to attend to, damage limitation to be attended to, and laundry to be done.

Aspire always to stay one step ahead of the game.

Attend to tasks as they arise as often as you can. In time you notice this is much less energy intensive than procrastinating and putting off.

Opening bank accounts as receptacles

At the time of writing, banks are still a relatively safe place to keep your currently excess money.

Open many bank (deposit) accounts, one to keep the earnings from one project; one to keep the earnings from another and so on.

Or you can have one account for building up the funds to buy your sanctuary, one as a fund for your dependants, one for building up funds for your retirement, one for building up funds to buy your recording facility, one for building up a charity fund and so on [see *Developing generosity* p.96]. These accounts become magnets for wealth.

Every day, visualise each account filling up with millions of units of money. Visualise your bank statements with five or six extra zeros.

Keep topping up each account whenever you can, if only with small amounts, leave the interest to sit and resist the temptation to deplete any of the accounts before time wherever possible.

Swindling and thieving

Resist all temptations to indulge in these activities, or by the immutable law of cause and effect, in time you will be thieved from or swindled yourself. And it always comes when it hurts the most.

By the same token, assume everyone with whom you have any kind of commerce is a potential thief and swindler who may not have such a highly developed appreciation of said immutable law.

This is not to advocate paranoia, but simply to remind you to be aware.

Watch everyone like a hawk. A compassionate, forgiving hawk, but a hawk none the less.

Pitching your price right

Resist the temptation to undersell yourself.

Underselling yourself is when you have an uncomfortable feeling around your 'tan tien', associated with low self-respect, coupled with feelings of resentment towards whoever you're underselling yourself.

Pitch the price you charge for your services/product as high as the market will bear during recessionary times and use this as a yardstick, not to be significantly exceeded during inflationary times (within reason).

Resist all temptations to be greedy. Greed results from fear. While motivated by fear, i.e. greed, your energy field contacts and diminishes, and thus loses its power to magnetise. This will result in a decrease in your fortunes.

The value of building a hunting team around you

As your project grows in size, you will need to build an effective support team around yourself.

When you're hunting for big game (deals/backing, etc.) you need a big team. You may need a business manager, agent, PR person/company, promotions company, accountant, lawyer, graphic designer, musical consultant, and even a cleaner. Going to market for a big pop, you're much more likely to be taken seriously with a heavyweight team around you.

If you're an artist of any kind, it is usually far more effective to have someone else sell your work for you. It's also more comfortable for the person you're selling to. Whenever attending important meetings, always have a member of your team present with you, if only for the extra bioplasmic and energetic mass, i.e. for emotional support. People tend to take you more seriously if they see others do too.

Do not be afraid of having to fork out money in commission payments to members of your indispensable team whenever appropriate. It's better to be left with only sixty, seventy or eighty per cent of something than be left with a hundred per cent of nought.

Working for no exchange

It is impossible to work, i.e. invest your time and energy in someone else, for no exchange.

It will always come back to you later. It may not come from the person in whom you invested, but it will definitely come from somewhere/one. However, when giving, give freely with no thought of returns. And then the returns will be truly pleasing. (But don't do it just for that!)

Importance of calculating skills

For purposes of effective negotiation skills, it is imperative that you be well versed in the simple operations of addition, subtraction, multiplication, division, fractions, decimals, percentages and ratios.

It is obviously preferable to be able to make these calculations rapidly and correctly, mentally or on paper. However, if you have problems in this area which you don't intend to rectify, at least carry a small calculator around with you and learn how to use it in such a way that you don't look like a prat.

Gambling

Resist the temptation to gamble on anything other than your own projects. Let these be your chips/lottery tickets. Every time you gamble otherwise or play the lottery, you're sending a message to your unconscious mind/higher self/Tao that you don't fully believe in your own self-created path. This makes a hole in your energy field/aura which weakens your ability to magnetise authentic f'n'f.

You say, 'Yes, but that fourteen million pounds would buy me my new recording studio. I could set up my own record company and fund my project properly, and if I play and win, it's because that's my Tao.'

And I say, 'Maybe.'

But I maintain that every time you gamble or play the lottery with intent suddenly and dramatically to change your life for the better, you're weakening your energetic abilities to manifest that change by your own hand.

I wager! Even if you win the lottery, the experience will prove ultimately anti-climactic and unfulfilling.

And if I'm wrong, you can call me pisher [see *Let them call you pisher* p.101].

Scud-dodging

This is private author stuff I wish to share with you.

I thought it would be romantic to finish this Handbook, i.e. press the final full-stop button on a Galilean hillside in northern Israel, where another barefoot nutter used to roam.

I've taught a few workshops (multitudes) in the Galilee myself, it's one of my touchbases. I thought it might add a few more degrees of spiritual factor to the atmosphere of the text. In any case, I had to get out of London, things were just too busy for me to think straight and I was developing a mild case of CPRP (cellular phone ringing phobia).

Thirty-six hours before flying to Tel Aviv from London, the United Nations, i.e. America, stood with missiles poised to splurge all over Iraq. The British Foreign Office was advising people not to travel to Israel. British tourists were being flown home. The British press was showing pictures of gas masks being handed out in Tel Aviv.

Except for Roya the Persian Queen, who probably thought a quick Scud on the head might knock some sense into me, and a couple of other diehard heroes, everyone I spoke to questioned the wisdom of my going. Aware that the news/propaganda machine was probably exaggerating the severity of the situation, I nevertheless felt the need to consult my pendulum.

The pendulum 'said', 'Go!'

So packing my crash helmet and acupuncture needles, I set off boldly on the fast train to the airport, where I had to sign a disclaimer. On arriving in Tel Aviv I was only mildly surprised to find that no one was displaying even a passing interest in the 'crisis' (the wily old dogs). A few hours later the crisis was diffused. (Nice theatre, boys.)

Right now, I'm sitting in a plush hotel bar on my way up north, overlooking a shiny blue Mediterranean, the 'world' temporarily at peace again.

Which goes to show three things:

I've got a very clever pendulum [see *Making decisions – pendulums, Tarot, I Ching* p.61).

You should always be prepared to take what you see on TV with a pinch of salt, i.e. never underestimate the power of propaganda.

A hero should never be deterred by the thought of a Scud from following his/her path.

Hero's prayer

To be spoken discreetly to your 'higher self', i.e. god of your choice.

'Give me the courage to follow my path to the death.
Give me the compassion to take care of others as I go.
Give me the intelligence always to tell myself the truth.
Give me an unwavering sense of humour.
Give me the wisdom not to seek fame or fortune.
Give me the sense to enjoy f'n'f and use them fruitfully when they come to me.
Let me always have access to an efficient accountant and a competent lawyer.
Let me always remember to feel gratitude for my life, no matter what.
Thank you.'

Toodeloo

Toodeloo, from the French, *toute a l'heure*, means until the next time.

Meanwhile, I've followed this trail of seventy thousand words, comprising approximately one and a half miles of text, having lost the odd few yards here and there by the occasional, inadvertent pressing of some mysterious wrong button and so having to redouble my efforts to rewrite and catch up, but finally here I stand, triumphant, on top of the mountain with only a couple more things to say from this high altitude.

If public opinion, wily beast that it is, turns against you, and it looks like your whole world, i.e. construct of reality, is crashing down upon your noble head, resist all temptations to engage in any rash or life-negating activities (suicide, turning to a life of drink, class-A drugs, violence or crime, etc.).

Simply keep the faith and hang in there till it all turns around, as it surely will. And if it doesn't you can call me pisher. (For the last time.)

And finally, concerning all this fame and fortune business, there is one last question you must ask yourself.

That is, '*Do I deserve it*?'

And the resounding answer is,'*Yes, I do*!'

Whatever the path you walk down. Walk with aplomb.

Toodeloo,

love,

Doc.

THANK YOU

All the people who helped make the passage of time during which *Handbook For Heroes* was conceived and written the fully magnificent experience it was. I can't include everyone whose light and love has touched me during this time, and pray forgiveness if you notice a deficiency of your name in the upcoming list of those who spring to mind before I whack in that last full stop, these being specifically:

Jamie Catto, JTFPS (Jamie-the-famous-pop-star), for your love, inspiration, encouragement, and elegantly delicate, on-the-road edit (brother).

Roya Arab, Persian Queen, voice of a thousand angels, for your love, biting wit and resisting urges to crown me with your skillet.

The Baron, Craig Newman, for your love, support and open-hearted joy in doing the business (thing) with such aplomb and finesse. The Baroness for loving and supporting the Baron and never cooking me dinner.

Danny Jacobsen, ultimate Zen Rabbi, for your love, timeless wisdom, mind-buggering insights *and* the character in the cupboard sitting there listening, also Yehudit, Mayan and Zohar for love and the deepest sleep in the forest.

Anat Dan-On (Astral Fumés), Heroine of the Himalayas, for your love, dervishness and guiding me to sanctuary in the Galilee.

Ojas, hero of heroes, for being so faultlessly so.

Russell Ward, Spiritual Firefighter, for your love, inspiration and full power (brother).

Antony Somers (Joio Ctoojaw/Nico Ramuda), ultimate flying-dude, for everything (master).

Heidi Easton (Phi Phi Rider, the perfect woman, PPTPW), for trusting your head in my hands, love and jollying up the aesthetics around here (fit thing).

Joe Russell, The Philosopher, for your love, ear, encouragement and consistently sardonic wit.

Jo Simons, Jo la Ho (meopath), for your love, ground support, remedies and unexpected angles.

Jake Russell, The Nobleman for your love, ear, generosity, wisdom, and pendulum swinging.

✦ thank you

Jonathon Champelovier, Jonty C, for your love, late-night existential conferences and sharing the graphic joys of life.

Michael Angelo Russell, Hero of the Caribbean, Captain of the Keys, for your love, support, poignant humour, inner/outer beauty and having such a lovely mum.

Claire Amerena and Mark Frumkes for the Floridian sojourn.

Desmond of Samui, for providing such a thick plot.

Betsy Rapoport and everyone at Times Books, New York, for such a classic meeting and hooking on to the Doc-plot.

Sally Clarke, PA to The Baron, global logistics coordinator, for taking command of the situation in your entertaining style and always making it fun to phone.

My mum and dad for standing by no matter what. (Someone has to.)

Zippi, the Soothsayer, for saying the sooth with such unabashed truth.

Di Di, the voice of choice, lord of the vocal chord, for looking after the Soothsayer (so vociferously).

Michelle Ziff, The Ziff, for love and keeping up the Lakshmi business.

Akbar Chouglay, for taking care of the numbers and being so gracious about it.

Karina Leapman, for protecting my person from danger so charmingly.

Karena Callen, for your love and support and for providing such an elegant example of truly beautiful womanhood.

Vanessa K, for your gracious space-control.

Sam K. for your kitchenly camaraderie.

Laurent, le Survivor, for your early-morning Frank Sinatra sessions.

Walter K, the Taoist Dog, for the late-night street patrols.

Kate Spicer (*Minx* magazine), for affording me the opportunity to speak to two hundred thousand naughty girls.

Judy Piatkus, Gill Cormode, Sandra Rigby, Philip Cotterel, Mel Harrison, Jana Sommerlad, Carol, the gentleman who answers the phone and everyone at Piatkus for entertaining such a wayward rascal as I.

Kary Stewart (Ig-nite PR), for your stalwart support, genuine enthusiasm, energy, integrity and tip-top PR work.

Paul Tully (Tullyman), for your friendship, support and watchful, brotherly eye.

Robbie Bear for smiling everywhere.

Dan Harrison, for your magnificent web-site design.

Mitch, for doing the chi (Ki) thing.

Swifty, for the Friday Tai Chi socials.

Cath, the Queen of West End Leene, for your love, support and bravery in the face of a mad, mad world.

Lisa Stemmer, the Helicopter Mistress, for your love, support and setting such a shining example of a shining example.

Philip Stemmer, Master of the Mouths-of-Others, for love and looking after the Helicopter Mistress and delightful brood.

Niel Spencer, for your unique mix of unbridled spirituality and rampant cynicism and for finally giving in and writing the astro book.

Meena Krishnamurty, most charming and beautiful of all medical doctors, for saving my life (literally).

Gabi Nitzan, Mcloed Gange Magician for making the charras disappear (and reappear) in Dharamkot.

Paul Bradshaw (Brad/Braders) for having the courage/madness to allow the Doctor to grace/disgrace the hallowed pages of Chaser.

Mickey, Hebron, Moses, Janine, Shekinah, Hallelulia, Shirley, Leat, Ronny and Ettie for facilitating the perfect dervish writing retreat at Amirey Hagalil (Upper Galilee) for the Wandering Doctor.

Ruthie Pavion, for your love warmth and north-country-style flying ground support.

Rowan O'Niel, Witch of America, for all your e-spells, divinations, humour in the face of death, love and magic(k).

Scott McHardy, (I say 'Mc', you say 'Mac'), you old seafaring dog – just for that.

Tamsin Lazarus, for shielding the Doctor from the fierce North wind on top of the hill.

Stevo Nakovitch, Ultimate Bad Boy, for teaching me everything you know.

The unfettered, all-absorbing unmentionable Tao, in all its complex majesty, for consistently coming up with such a damn good show.

The guy who runs the service department at Psion, for replacing my collapsing Psion 5 with a fresh one free of charge, upon which I then wrote this entire book (it's true).

Jason, Queen of New York City, just 'cause I love you and for the shower gel.

Patria C Barbary, my Cosmic God-Mother, for helping bring out the hero in the Doctor.

Yehudi Gordon, The Great Doctor Himself, for proving you *can* get younger while you're busy getting older.

Susanna Greenwood, hypnotherapy mistress, for hypnotising me into writing the entire first draft of this book in seventeen days flat.

Edie Freeman, for all the remedial vists and keeping me functioning.

G.L.O.R.I.A. Else, for love, ground support and keeping the tunes topped up.

Peter Williams, The Dancing Lens Master, for sub-flyover tequila lunacy and master-shots.

Mary Wier, Queen of Scots and Kentish Town, for being an unshakeable pillar of goodness and love.

Richard Cannon, for your love, outdoor Easy Rider experience and the Barefeet in Oxford Street event.

Pat Wier, for keeping the rolling stock rolling and giving me the maddest surprise of the year.

Lucky Luke, for all the hours.

Max Patel, just because you're lovely and how could I not include you in such a gathering?

Ganesha The Elephant God, for clearing all obstacles from my path.

The ex-Frank Kramer, Dead Hero, for continuing to be as good a friend from that side as you were from this.

The ex-R.D. Laing, Dead Ultra-Hero, for taking me on twenty-two years ago.

You, the reader, for deigning to play the reader/author game with the Mad Doctor.

And finally, me, the Mad Doctor, for being so much fun to work with, I'm beginning to think we should do this more often.

Cheers.

Visit Barefoot Doctor's Worldwide Healing website at
www.barefootdoctor.co.uk

INDEX